The Truth About Law School

What You Need to Know Before You Commit

Rachel B. Wickenheiser

The Truth About Law School
Copyright © 2022 by Rachel B. Wickenheiser
Philadelphia, Pa.

ISBN: 978-0-578-28684-6 (Paperback)
ISBN: 978-0-578-29815-3 (eBook)

Library of Congress Control Number: 2022908144

Printed in the United States of America

Are You Ready for Law School?

Take the free quiz to find out!

As a thank you for downloading my book, I'd like to help you figure out if you're truly ready for law school.

I've found that there is often too much emphasis on the admissions process and not enough on what comes after, so I've created a short quiz to see how prepared you are.

Click the link below to find out if you're ready for the challenge!

To take the quiz, go to:
subscribepage.io/truthaboutlawschool

Follow me on social media:
@rachelbwick

Table of Contents

Table of Contents

Introduction: Why You Need This Book

In 2011, I graduated from Harvard Law School. The road to get there wasn't pretty (more on that later), but I survived.

This is not a book about how to get into law school. This is a book about what to do if you're thinking about law school... but there's a tiny, niggling seed of doubt.

Unfortunately, there is a serious lack of information about what law school — and for that matter, practicing law — is actually like. The reason is that the people who know what law school is like have no incentive to tell you. The biggest culprits are law schools and colleges. Law schools don't want to tell you because they want your money. And colleges don't want to tell you because they want lots of their students going on to grad school so they look good. The rest of the people who know the truth are lawyers themselves, but they either have too much on their plate to go out of their way to tell you or simply don't know the best way to communicate their hard-earned wisdom.

That's why I decided to write this book. I hate that law schools are continuing to take advantage of people who don't know any better. And I want you to know what you're getting into before you take on the physical, mental, and financial hardships of law school.

Here are some examples of what I'll be covering:

- The rampant mental health issues in the legal profession;

- Why the comfortingly high employment statistics offered by law schools are misleading; and

- What to do if you're still hell-bent on going to law school.

But why should you listen to me? First, on a superficial level, I have a fairly impressive resume: after Harvard, I scored a federal clerkship, worked at two prestigious law firms, and then moved over to the federal government. After serving as a pre-law advisor and teaching undergraduate law classes at a state university, I now work outside law but coach law school applicants on the side. In short, I've gotten to see law from several different angles, which in turn has allowed me to gain a fuller picture of the challenges and questions that aspiring lawyers face.

Second, I interviewed over a dozen lawyers (and former lawyers) about what they're doing now and what they wish they had done differently, which I've incorporated throughout the book. I've also done a ton of secondary research — there will be the footnotes throughout, and you'll find a list of references at the end.

Now, before we go any further, my name-dropping 'Harvard Law School' may make some of you wonder if this book is right for you, especially if you think you won't be able to get into a top-tier school.

The answer is YES. While there are some substantive differences between tiers of law schools (which I'll discuss where relevant), even more things are universal.

So let's dive in.

Prologue: An Extremely Brief History of U.S. Law (and Why It Matters)

Before we get to the realities of being a lawyer, a quick overview of the legal system in the United States is necessary to understand why it's dysfunctional. The problems in the legal profession didn't just spring from nowhere; a lot of it is due to how U.S. law is set up.

Common law vs. civil law

Like the UK and all its former colonies, the U.S. has a common law system, which means laws are interpreted based on the precedents set by prior court decisions. As you might guess, if a judge wants to rule differently from a previous case, it can lead to the judge awkwardly maneuvering around the facts to distinguish it from the earlier case, leading to a body of convoluted and impenetrable case law that will make future lawyers want to tear their hair out. And I won't even get into the myriad and conflicting theories about how law should be interpreted in the first instance.

So what is the alternative to common law? The major one is civil law, which is what most of Europe has. (If you're wondering, the UK ended up with a different system because of William the Conquerer.)

Civil law means each judge interprets the text of laws independently, without being bound by what previous judges have said. I'll be honest, I don't know how much this is abided by in practice, but it saves you from being formally constrained by ridiculous or sloppy opinions, if the earlier judges didn't clearly explain their reasoning, or their reasoning is just plain faulty or based on outdated norms (you know, like racism).

Sure, there's a certain element of chaos in civil law too, in that the outcome appears to be entirely dependent on the judge you get, but that's pretty much the case in common law too. Just look at the U.S. Supreme Court: If interpreting the law is a neutral, objective endeavor, then why can we accurately predict how the justices will rule 99% if the time? Civil law seems far better to me than a system in which judges end up distinguishing similar cases by weak, warped, or imaginary rationales, which other courts are then stuck with.

Law vs. equity

Back in the day in England, there were two different court systems: courts of law and courts of equity. Aside from a few holdouts, like Delaware's Court of Chancery, the courts of equity have mostly been swallowed up by the courts of law, leading to our current legal system.

Why does this matter?

Equity allowed a court to do what seemed right (or, dare I say it, equitable) in the specific context of the situation. In contrast, the legal system requires doing whatever the applicable law says, even if it seems unfair in the immediate situation. Sure, some principles of equity have survived, like unclean hands (which means you can't benefit from your own wrongdoing), but aside from a few areas like family law and bankruptcy, the courts have made clear that equity is always the last resort. In other words, room for flexibility and fairness in law has largely been eradicated.

At this point, that seed of doubt might be sprouting. If so, the good news is that you haven't actually committed yourself to entering this profession yet. If you're still feeling cautiously optimistic, keep reading.

Part One:

The Myth of Law School

Chapter 1: Why Do You Want to Go to Law School?

Too many people (myself included) go to law school for the wrong reasons. Will Meyerhofer, a former lawyer who is now a psychotherapist and blogger known as the People's Therapist, says that he went to law school "for the usual reasons. I didn't have anything else to do, and my mother wouldn't leave me alone — I received nagging phone calls on a daily basis in which she lectured me on how I needed 'a graduate degree' to succeed in the world. I had a high LSAT score and good grades from Harvard, and law seemed to be what people did when they had good grades and didn't know what else to do — it promised money and prestige without much effort."

Most college students who go straight to law school end up there because they're smart and reasonably articulate, they don't have skills and/or interest in math or science, and maybe they took a couple of law-related classes and liked them. (We'll talk about law-related clubs in a sec.)

They might also be terrified by the prospect of entering the real world, especially when they contemplate their bachelor's degree in medieval French history. Or maybe they just have no idea what they would *do* after college, and law school seems like a safe and obvious choice. They like the idea of the prestige of being a lawyer, and have been told by some well-meaning non-lawyer that "there's so much you can do with a law degree."

If you go to law school for these reasons:

1. Welcome to the club.

2. It's still the wrong reason even if that's why most people go. (Enter your mom saying, "And if everyone else jumped off a bridge, would you do it too?")

3. You will most likely be funneled down the path to a big law firm if you're "lucky," or unemployed and saddled with debt if you're not.

Or maybe you're thinking to yourself, "No, I definitely *want* to go to law school." Okay, great. Why?

If you say anything along the lines of, "Because I like *Law & Order* and love to argue," I forbid you to go to law school.

If you have the more reasonable response of, "I've done some law-related stuff, which I liked, and I'm interested in [insert type of law here]," that's more promising, but I'm still skeptical. Do you know what it's like to actually practice that type of law? Have you spoken with or, even better, worked with any lawyers who practice that type of law?

If you have, excellent! And if not, make that your #1 priority. Reading stuff on the internet doesn't count — I'm talking live interaction, in person or over the phone. Don't make the same mistakes I did.

When I applied to law school, I thought I wanted to work in the Civil Rights Division of the U.S. Department of Justice. My law school admissions essay was about my interest in civil rights. You know how much civil rights work I've actually done? Almost none. That's because I had no idea what practicing civil rights law actually entailed, and once I found out more during my transition from private to public practice, I wasn't as interested.

Law school is just too expensive, and too much work, not to do your research before you commit. And if you haven't spent any significant length of time with lawyers outside of television and movies, you're not ready to commit.

Since doing my first Mock Trial in middle school, I "knew" that I wanted to be a lawyer. I was good at writing and public speaking, I received positive feedback and opportunities through Mock Trial, and I won awards doing Model Congress, Model U.N., and all that other stuff that privileged kids who think they're probably going to law school do in high school. I'm not saying this to brag, but just to illustrate how obvious it seemed at the time that I should become a lawyer, and how irrelevant it actually was.

In college, I took a detour. I dutifully went to the first meeting for college-level Mock Trial, but never went back. While part of it was because the initial meeting was huge and disorganized (always a turn-off for my type-A personality), it also seemed a *lot* more difficult than high school-level Mock Trial.

So instead, I spent a lot of time doing theater and other random activities. I told myself, "Since I already know I'm going to law school, I might as well do other things while I can."

In hindsight, my lack of interest should have been a clue. Not because Mock Trial accurately represents what it's like to be a lawyer (it doesn't), but because I was already finding the procedural complexity of college-level Mock Trial boring. And trust me, it gets exponentially worse in real practice. (If you don't believe me, start reading the Federal Rules of Civil Procedure and see how many rules you can get through before you want to jump off a cliff.)

Towards the end of college, I started going to pre-law events, where I learned that few lawyers actually go to trial, and of those, *very* few do so on a regular basis. But I figured that was no big deal, since I liked writing, which was apparently most of what lawyers did, and I enjoyed the analytical thinking and building a case that I had done in Mock Trial.

Later on, I would discover that the day-to-day life of a lawyer bears almost no resemblance to anything I had done in high school: I spent most of my time alone in my office, researching and writing, with little say in the cases that I got assigned to, and certainly no control over my work schedule. But when I was nearing the end of college, I didn't know any lawyers who could tell me what it was really like, and I couldn't handle the panic I felt every time I thought about what I would do if I *didn't* go to law school.

Long story short, I had no idea what I was getting into, even though I thought I did. And if this has made you realize you don't have an answer to why you want to go to law school (aside from parental expectations, being a high achiever, and/or a lack of knowledge about other options), it's time to sit down and reevaluate.

Chapter 2: What Being a Lawyer Is Not

There are many sources of misconception about what being a lawyer is like. Some culprits are obvious, like television and movies. But other sources are less obvious, like family expectations — "they want this for me and think I deserve it, therefore it must be good and desirable" — and even school activities like Mock Trial. Collectively, they paint an unrealistic picture of what lawyers' lives are like. In truth, there are very few trial lawyers, but since they're disproportionately represented in popular culture, there's a shroud of mystery around what the rest of lawyers do.

Hopefully this goes without saying, but pop culture (T.V. shows, movies, novels, etc.) does not accurately depict what being a lawyer is like. Neither do theoretically-law-related activities like Mock Trial. Why not? First of all, there are a hell of a lot more procedural rules in real practice, which will drive you bonkers, even if you generally love rules and guidelines.

Second, in real trial work, the fact record is way messier and more complicated. You don't get a neat little packet of materials. You're the one gathering and compiling the materials from all the case debris you have to wade through. And unlike Mock Trial, there's no guarantee that the case will be evenly balanced so that each side can make a decent argument.

Third, because you're young and trying your best, and because the attorneys and judges in Mock Trial are a self-selected group of folks who are volunteering because they want to encourage you, they're going to be much nicer to you than real judges are to real lawyers. Seeing how tyrannical and harsh some judges are in real life was a rude awakening for me, and not something I particularly wanted to subject myself to.

Finally, as I mentioned above, few attorneys spend significant time in court. Instead, most lawyers spend their time doing discovery (which is generally boring and horrible), drafting various legal documents (many of which are technical and not that interesting), and, if the lawyers are more senior, talking to clients and/or opposing counsel (who are often annoying).

I'll talk about all of this in more detail as we go, but I wanted to note this at the outset to get you thinking about the invisible scripts in your life that have steered you towards law school. Being a lawyer is not glamorous. So if you have *any* doubts about going to law school, carve out space and time for yourself to think it through. It's just too damn much work otherwise.

Chapter 3: What Is a J.D. Good For?

There are very few jobs that you *need* a J.D. for. I've compiled a fairly exhaustive list. It is short.

Jobs you need a J.D. for:

- Being an actual, practicing lawyer
- Becoming a judge
- Becoming a law professor
- Becoming a legal recruiter
- Becoming a law school career counselor
- Working at a legal publication like Bloomberg BNA

Jobs you don't need a J.D. for:

- Pretty much everything else.

If someone — like, say, a well-meaning parent — says, "But you can do so much with a law degree," chances are they are not a lawyer.[1] If that happens, simply ask, "Like what?" Odds are, they will be at a loss before eventually stammering, "Uh... politics?" At which point, if you really want

---

[1] Jim Saksa, "'You Can Do Anything With a Law Degree,'"*Slate*, May 14, 2014, https://slate.com/human-interest/2014/05/you-can-do-anything-with-a-law -degree-no-no-you-cannot.html.

to be mean, you can say, "But I don't *need* a law degree to get into politics, right?" (More on politics in a sec.)

Yes, there is some variety within the legal profession, but you definitely need to have a more concrete idea of what your options are than just the vague notion that you can do "so much" with a law degree. Law school may open doors, but it also closes others. As one interviewee, Lisa, puts it, "There's a myth that a law degree doesn't limit your options, but it *does*."

Lawyers are trained to be risk averse. After all, if you take risks, you're leaving yourself open to liability, and it's the lawyer's job to minimize that. But, as Lisa discovered, that doesn't necessarily translate well outside of the legal world. After leaving law, Lisa went to work at a Silicon Valley company, where she observed that "[l]awyers are broadly perceived to be more risk-averse than folks from other industries. There's also a healthy skepticism of lawyers' general abilities to adjust towards less hierarchical or structured organizations."

So unless you have your heart set on one of the six careers above — AND you've talked to at least three people who actually have that job — there is probably another path that doesn't require years of sweat and tears and hundreds of thousands of dollars of debt.

Jobs in the gray area

There are two jobs that deserve special mention, where a J.D. isn't necessary but it is common:

1. Consulting. I interviewed at McKinsey, a prominent consulting firm, when I was looking for a job my 3L year. McKinsey actually specifically recruits lawyers so that, as they put it during my interview, they have people who can write in complete sentences.

As I learned the hard way, you also need an intermediate understanding of economics. I had a basic understanding of economics, having taken two economics courses in college (thus enabling me to throw around terms like "opportunity cost," which we'll get to later), but it wasn't enough. When it came to the multiple-choice test, I didn't even understand most of the questions.

The other thing you have to be able to do is problem-solve in a business-oriented way, which is tough to do as a law student, because you're usually not really trained for that (although you should be, since law is a business as much as it is a profession). Unfortunately for me, there was a JD/MBA joint-degree student in my group of interviewees who blew us JD-only nerds out of the water.

2. Politics. It turns out that 26 of the 46 U.S. presidents, or 56.5%, have been lawyers. That means that roughly half *haven't* been.

Moreover, according to a 2015 study,[2] the percentage of lawyers in Congress has been steadily *declining* since the mid-nineteenth century, from about 80% to just under 40% in the 114th Congress.[3] The author, Nick Robinson, argues that this is due to the rise of a "specialized political class," combined with the "increasingly professionalized and commercialized work environment" of law.[4] Whether or not that theory is correct, the point is that you don't need a law degree to go into politics.

---

[2] Nick Robinson, "The Decline of the Lawyer-Politician," *Buffalo Law Review* 65, no. 4 (August 2017): 657-737.

[3] Robinson, 659.

[4] Robinson, 659-60.

Part Two:

What You Don't Know About Law School Could Hurt You

Chapter 4: Losing Yourself

Becoming a lawyer fundamentally changes you, because it changes how you think — you can't turn the lawyer off. You become even more risk-averse, more pessimistic (since lawsuits generally arise out of people screwing each other over), and most importantly, you forget how to be a person. You forget that there are other things to life besides law. And what does that make you? Boring as hell. Except to other lawyers, of course.

Case in point: A friend from law school was dating someone from a nearby medical school. Eventually, she noticed that they were always hanging out with his friends. "How come we never hang out with my friends?" she asked him. "Because your friends only talk about law," he replied. Some of you might think this guy is just a jerk, but trust me, he's not wrong.

Law school has a way of hijacking your identity. For instance, one empirical study found that law students were "disturbed by the sense of isolation and alienation from their former selves."[5] Similarly, Daisy Hurst Floyd, a law professor

---

[5] Molly Townes O'Brien, Stephen Tang, and Kath Hall, "Changing Our Thinking: Empirical Research on Law Student Wellbeing, Thinking Styles and the Law Curriculum," *Legal Education Review* 21, no. 2 (January 2011): 180.

and former dean of Mercer University School of Law, observes:

> The law school culture values the cognitive, rational, and analytical to the almost total exclusion of other qualities. The result is a devaluing of everything else, including emotional matters, relationships, and students' ethical and moral values.[6]

This personal transformation in learning to "think like a lawyer" has been correlated with the rampant mental health issues I mentioned in the introduction.[7] Mental health issues among law students and lawyers are a well-known problem within the legal profession that aspiring law students don't discover until they're already in the thick of it, since it's not

---

[6] Daisy Hurst Floyd, "We Can Do More," *Journal of Legal Education* 60, no. 1 (August 2010): 131. *See also* Kennon M. Sheldon and Lawrence S. Krieger, "Does Legal Education Have Undermining Effects on Law Students? Evaluating Changes in Motivation, Values, and Well-Being," *Behavioral Sciences and the Law* 22 (2004); "Making Docile Lawyers: An Essay on the Pacification of Law Students," *Harvard Law Review* 111 (1998): 2030 ("[B]y the end of the first year, law students have learned to maintain a detached attitude toward the law, and consequently become alienated from their former ideals.").

[7] *See* O'Brien, et al., "Changing Our Thinking"; Sheldon & Krieger, "Does Legal Education Have Undermining Effects on Law Students?"; Elizabeth Mertz, *The Language of Law School: Learning to "Think Like a Lawyer"* (New York: Oxford University Press, 2007).

exactly like law schools are advertising the fact. Some facts and figures:

- Upon entering law school, law students have a rate of depression commensurate with the general population. But by the time they graduate, 20-40% of law students are depressed and/or have some other psychological dysfunction.[8] In other words, **something about law school actually *makes* people depressed**.

- Lawyers are 3.6 times more likely to suffer from depression than people in other occupations.[9]

- Lawyers also rank highest for loneliness compared to other professions.[10]

On top of that, the legal profession cares more about appearances and perceived prestige than about what actually makes sense. For instance, the higher-ranked the law

[8] Rhodes, "Legal Education," 36; G. Andrew H. Benjamin et al., "The Role of Legal Education in Producing Psychological Distress Among Law Students and Lawyers," *American Bar Foundation Research Journal* 11, no. 2 (Spring 1986): 246.

[9] William W. Eaton et al., "Occupations and the Prevalence of Major Depressive Disorder." *Journal of Occupational Medicine* 32, no. 11 (Nov. 1990): 1085.

[10] Shawn Achor, *et al.*, "America's Loneliest Workers, According to Research," *Harvard Business Review*, March 19, 2018, https://hbr.org/2018/03/americas-loneliest-workers-according-to-research.

school, the less practical stuff you learn, probably because your professors are more likely to be academics instead of people who have actually practiced law. And *everything*, from law schools to firms to clerkships,[11] has a ranking. Appellate clerkships are more prestigious than trial clerkships, federal is more prestigious than state, big firms are more prestigious than small ones, and so on.

It's disturbingly easy to get sucked into the pretense. In college, I had done whatever extracurricular activities sounded interesting, and it was amazing. In contrast, once I got to law school, I was steered toward doing what "looked good" on my resume, because (a) everyone else was doing it, and (b) unlike college, there were clear specifications regarding what "looked good." It "looked good" to be on a journal, it "looked good" to take XYZ classes, it "looked good" to intern at the DOJ instead of a small no-name agency if you wanted to go into government.

And in doing what "looked good," I lost track of who I was and what I wanted. The problem with that — aside from being miserable — is that once you're a few years out of law school, it becomes exponentially harder to change tracks because you're seen as only being able to do whatever you landed in after law school. For instance, if you ended up

---

[11] I'll talk about what clerkships are in Ch. 10 (Life in Other Legal Environments).

doing bankruptcy work after law school, congratulations, you're now a bankruptcy lawyer. So good luck applying for that environmental law job.

Besides setting you up to be unhappy in your career, there is another, even more insidious aspect to "looking good": feeling like you have to hide any sign of weakness. This is referred to as duck syndrome — the idea being that, while it appears like the duck is floating peacefully on the water, under the surface the duck is paddling frantically.

I never experienced duck syndrome, so I'm not sure what it's like to actually have it, though I imagine it's lonely and exhausting. It also seems like those folks are the ones who are most at risk for serious mental health issues. For instance, the Dave Nee Foundation, whose mission is to eliminate the stigma associated with depression and suicide, was founded after its namesake, Dave Nee, committed suicide a month after graduating from Fordham Law School in 2005. His suicide came as a shock to his family and friends because no one had any idea that he was suffering from depression. After all, Dave was a star on the law school's moot court team and was otherwise doing well in school.

In a blog post, Rachael Barrett, then the Executive Director of the Dave Nee Foundation, mentioned that a common response she receives from lawyers to Dave's story is "maybe Dave shouldn't have been in law school because clearly, he couldn't handle the stress."[12]

Putting aside the ignorance about depression this response demonstrates, the bigger problem is that it puts the onus entirely on Dave to have dealt with the stress and his ensuing mental health issues. According to this view (which is emblematic of the legal profession as a whole), being a lawyer is all about personal failure or success, without any compassion or willingness to help each other, let alone acknowledgement of the possibility that maybe it shouldn't be that stressful to begin with. Unfortunately, it's easy to lose sight of how unrealistic the expectations are when you feel as though everything hinges solely on keeping up with everyone else.

In addition to potential mental health issues, there can be physical side effects to law school. One unexpected example is eyesight. In the years preceding law school, my vision had gotten worse by just a half step every year, so I only needed a new prescription every other year. But a mere *four months* into law school, my vision got worse by not one, not two, but three "steps" (known as diopters). I brought my new prescription to the eyeglass store, and the woman looked at

---

[12] Jeena Cho, "How to Know Suicide," *Above the Law,* March 31, 2015, http://abovethelaw.com/2015/03/how-to-know-suicide/.

it, compared it to my old one from four months ago, and said, "Are you sure?"

Yes, I was sure. In fact, two different optometrists I visited later commented on how common it was for law students' vision to deteriorate during law school.

And pleasure reading? Forget about it. Law school will crush any desire to read for fun. During my first week at law school, I was talking to a 3L and mentioning some novels that I had read recently. She said, "Yeah... I don't really read for fun anymore." I couldn't fathom such a thing. But sure enough, as law school got underway, I didn't have time to read anything other than case law. And on the rare occasions I did have free time, my eyes were too tired, as was my brain.

I remember one glorious day after my finals when I took a trip to the public library. As I made the trek back to campus, I ran into a fellow law student who wasn't done with finals yet. After we exchanged greetings and engaged in the obligatory griping about finals, he looked at the books in my hand, and said accusingly, "Is that ... pleasure reading? I hate you." He was joking. But not really.

And yes, I struggled with depression as well. Prior to law school, I had always loved school and been at the top of my class. But law school was different. I didn't like the work, and I wasn't very good at "thinking like a lawyer," at least the way law school defined it. But my mom (not a lawyer) wanted me to stay in, and I told myself that I should stick it out, since I had heard — I have no idea where — that practicing law was more enjoyable than law school. The other thing that kept me in law school was that I had no idea what else I would do if I did drop out, and unfortunately, that fear of the unknown proved stronger than my hatred of law school.

So I stayed, and during that time, I was formally diagnosed with clinical depression. I cried a lot, because my future as a lawyer was becoming increasingly clear and I did not like what I saw.

Sure, your experience might be different. But remember: something about law school actually *makes* people depressed and feel alienated from their former selves and ideals. How can you know that you'll be an exception?

Chapter 5: The Mechanics of Law School

All right, let's talk about what you actually *do* in law school.

Classes

First, the classes. Aside from some exceptions I'll talk about later in this chapter, law school bears little resemblance to practicing law. In fact, that's what got me through law school: I hated law school with a burning passion, but I stuck it out in the hopes that actually practicing law would be better. Conversely, this divergence caused a friend of mine to leave law after practicing for a few years — she had loved law school, but didn't like practicing law because it was completely different.

The point of law school is to teach you to "think like a lawyer." That means: (a) issue-spotting (i.e., being given a set of facts and determining the potential legal issues), and (b) analyzing those issues based entirely on what the case law says, regardless of your intuition or moral values or sense of justice. (Maybe this would be less onerous if courts were consistent, but believe me, they aren't.) However, most law classes don't teach you how to be a lawyer, just like learning grammar doesn't teach you how to write well.

And if you've done any kind of research on law school before picking up this book, you've probably heard of the "Socratic method." This is where the professor randomly calls on students to answer questions. It's definitely nerve-wracking: my heart raced every time the professor looked down at the list to pick their next victim, as I prayed that I had read all the cases closely enough to answer the professor's nitpicky questions.

But I don't consider this anywhere near the worst part of law school. This is partly because few professors use pure Socratic method anymore, and partly because no one is listening to you anyway since they're surfing the internet (unless you're not prepared and the professor calls you out on it, in which case people are definitely listening).

Besides, most of the class time will be taken up by "gunners." Gunners are students who think so highly of their own opinions that they just have to share them with the whole class. (Or else they're just trying to impress the professor and don't care if the rest of the class is giving them the evil eye.) They're also the jerks who will raise their hand to ask a long-winded question right at the end of class and haunt professors' office hours to make sure the professor knows who they are and how "smart" they are. Theoretically, they're also obsessed with getting the top grades in all their classes, but since I wasn't friends with any gunners, I can neither confirm nor deny. Anyway, yeah, no one likes them.

You'll take the core courses your first year of law school: Civil Procedure, Property, Contracts, Torts, Criminal Law, and maybe Criminal Procedure and Constitutional Law. These are usually large lecture classes with the same 80 or so classmates. You'll also take at least one year of legal writing and research. Even though this is the most useful and practical course you will take, it is worth the least amount of credit and is usually taught by an adjunct at the bottom of the faculty food chain. So that's nice.

After your first year, you can generally pick your courses, although there are "recommended" electives, like Corporations and Federal Courts. (I have no idea who actually does the recommending — you just learn the expectations through osmosis.) Those electives also tend to be large lecture classes, but you can sign up for smaller, discussion-based seminars as well. You can also enroll in clinicals, which I'll talk more about later in this chapter.

Now, you may have heard about the absurd amount of work in law school. As hinted earlier when I mentioned my deteriorating vision and lack of time or energy for fun reading, the rumors are 100% true. You're assigned to read several cases a night per class, and for every assigned case, you have to know all the pieces: the parties, the facts, the procedural history, the court's holdings, its reasoning, and any dissents or concurring opinions. So you need to study each case in excruciating detail.

In class, random students will be interrogated about the cases, and after dissecting each case in mind-numbing detail, discussion will turn to the legal theory underlying the cases. Which may not sound that bad, but remember what I said about law school hijacking your identity in teaching you how to "think like a lawyer"?[13] This is how they do it: by fixating on rational analysis at the expense of everything else.[14]

But human beings aren't designed to be totally rational all the time. Your intuitions about right and wrong? Not rational. (Yes, you can rationalize them, but that's not the same thing.) So that sense of justice compelling you to go to law school might well get eradicated when you're actually at law school.

Think I'm exaggerating? One study surveyed students at Florida State University College of Law throughout their three years there: once at the beginning of 1L year, again at the end of 1L year, and then midway through their 2L and 3L years.[15] Over the course of their first year, students who started law school with the aim of helping people stopped

---

[13] Technically, only correlation, not causation, has been shown, but the inference is pretty strong.

[14] *See* O'Brien et al. (2011), 167-168; Floyd, "We Can Do More," *Journal of Legal Education* 60, no. 1 (August 2010): 131; Lawrence S. Krieger, "Human Nature as a New Guiding Philosophy for Legal Education and the Profession," *Washburn Law Journal* 47 (2008): 265-266. *See also* Joshua E. Perry, "Thinking Like a Professional," *Journal of Legal Education* 58 (2008): 159-165.

[15] Kennon M. Sheldon and Lawrence S. Krieger, "Does Legal Education Have Undermining Effects on Law Students? Evaluating Changes in Motivation, Values, and Well-Being," *Behavioral Sciences and the Law* 22 (2004): 267.

caring about that and instead started placing more importance on appearance.[16]

As if that weren't bad enough, during their second and third years, those law students stopped caring much about *anything*.[17] Essentially, when asked what they cared most about — everything from friends and personal growth to money and fame — they were like, "I dunno."

These law students are not aberrations. They're just normal people who went to law school. So if you think you'd be different, think long and hard about why you're special.

Final exams

At the end of classes, of course, there are the finals. For most classes, your final exam is the *only grade* you get. There are exceptions, of course, but they're few and far between, especially for those traditional classes like Tax and Evidence. Plus, classes are generally graded on a curve, so by definition, not everyone can do well. No pressure.

On top of that, every law school has some version of an obscenely long take-home final exam. At Harvard, it's an 8-hour exam. And believe me, you're working every minute of

---

[16] Sheldon & Krieger, "Does Legal Education Have Undermining Effects on Law Students?", 272-273.
[17] Sheldon & Krieger, 274.

those 8 hours. Have you ever run on adrenaline and anxiety for 8 hours straight? It's not fun.

Usually, you're given one or more fact patterns (that's lawyerspeak for a description of what's happened in a real or hypothetical case), which will incorporate elements borrowed and modified from the cases you've studied during the semester. You have to spot the potential legal issues (remember "issue-spotting"?) and figure out if the professor's modifications are legally significant.

And on top of just trying to get through the exam while making sure you don't miss any issues, there are usually word limits. So after you finish the issue-spotting and analysis, you have to go back and figure out what you can cut out without potentially damaging your grade.

At the end of my first semester, I had two 8-hour exams with a single day in between. I almost vomited at the end of the second exam because my body couldn't take the constant stress anymore. I know some people who had back-to-back 8-hour exams, and I honestly have no idea how they survived.

Other law schools, like the George Washington University and Georgetown University, have 24-hour exams. I'm not sure if this is better or worse. I'm fairly confident the gunners wouldn't sleep at all, but it's unclear what the expectations would be for everyone else. I did read an article by a

Georgetown 1L saying that she took time off to go play soccer with friends during her 24-hour exam, which I hope that's what most folks do instead of hunching in front of their laptop all day...

Extracurricular activities

"Don't law students do *anything* for fun?" you ask plaintively. Well, many of them drink a lot. There's something called Bar Review where the whole point is to go out and drink a lot with your fellow law students (lawyers do love their legal puns), but given the disproportionately high rate of alcoholism in the legal profession,[18] I wouldn't recommend it as a coping mechanism.

---

[18] In a 2016 national study, 36.4% of lawyers scored positive for alcohol abuse or dependence, based on quantity and frequency of use. For comparison, 15.4% of surgeons — another high-pressure profession — scored positive in another study using the same measure.

Which is to say, lawyers are more than twice as likely to be alcoholics as people facing the enormous pressure of actually saving lives.

Patrick R. Krill, Ryan Johnson, and Linda Albert, "The Prevalence of Substance Use and Other Mental Health Concerns Among American Attorneys," *Journal of Addiction Medicine* 10, no. 1 (January/February 2016): 51; Michael R. Oreskovich, Krista L. Kaups, Charles M. Balch, et al. "Prevalence of Alcohol Use Disorders Among American Surgeons." *Arch Surgery* 147, no. 2 (2012): 170.

When I went to the extracurricular activities fair my 1L year, almost everything was law-related. I think that's when I began to realize that I didn't like law enough to do it 24/7.

The only things not law-related were Harvard Law Society (for those law students trying to recreate their college Greek life; unsurprisingly, they also organize Bar Review), sports, and theater. Even the a cappella group — Scales of Justice, naturally — did nothing but law-related parodies of songs. Did I mention lawyers love legal puns?

Special mention: Law reviews and journals

Speaking of extracurriculars, one striking example of the absurdity of law school is the "importance" of being on law review or some other secondary journal. Practically speaking, it's pointless if you're not going into academia, aside from the fact that you'll be decent at using the Bluebook from your many hours of checking citations.

Oh, the Bluebook. While innocuous on its face, it symbolizes the painstaking misery of law school.

The Bluebook is a citation manual, the legal world's version of the Chicago Manual of Style or MLA Handbook. When you first join a journal, your job is to check the citations, both for substance and formatting, in an article that the journal is going to publish. To do this cite-checking, you and a bunch of other sad souls on the journal gather in the library once a semester for what is called a "subcite" or "spading." During these subcites, everyone sits around silently checking citations *for the entire day.*

After one of these subcites, I wanted to drop out of law school. I mean, it wasn't just because of that, but it was definitely the straw that broke the camel's back. That's how horrible and mind-numbing subcites are.

But don't take my word for it. In writing this chapter, I couldn't remember the word "subcite" (probably because my brain was trying to protect me), so I posted the question on Facebook. One friend commented, "I thought it was called purgatory." Another remarked, "I call it 'that thing I did once and then decided life was too short.'"

Law review is the most prestigious journal at each school, and it's usually the only one that you actually have to try out for. At Harvard, the competition takes place over one grueling week after the spring semester ends, and unlike the Georgetown 1L who took a break from her 24-hour exam to play soccer, you're literally working the entire week. That is, if you don't burn out and give up, which happens to a decent chunk of participants each year.

At the beginning of the competition, you get a massive packet of paper (and by "massive," I mean roughly *one thousand* pages) and two assignments. For the first assignment, you have to draft a mock case comment based on a prompt, using only the sources in one of the packets. In the second, you get a shoddy draft of a law review article and have to edit it for both technical errors (using the trusty ol' Bluebook) and for larger substantive issues like structure and organization.

You find out your results around July. If you "won" and made it onto law review, you have to come back one or two weeks early to do ... law review stuff. Which, to be honest, I don't know much about besides the fact that it involves editing and cite-checking legal articles. But I do know that you will probably never see your friends from 1L year ever again, because you will be spending all of your waking hours in Gannett House (or whatever the equivalent of law review home base is at other law schools).

For instance, a friend of mine made it onto law review, and even though we lived on the same floor for all three years of law school, I basically never saw her again. As another example, a different friend of mine was dating someone on law review, and she recounted a time, by no means unusual, when the law review folks took a *break* at 3 AM to play video games.

Long story short, getting onto law review is like a pie-eating contest where the prize is more pie.

So why does anyone do it? First, as I mentioned before, it's prestigious as hell. Graduating during the Great Recession, everyone in my class was having trouble finding a job — except for the kids on law review. Most of us got 1-3 interviews, while they were getting upwards of 15. (Granted, even 1-3 interviews was more than what kids at lower-tier schools were getting during the recession, but still. What's the point of going to Harvard if job security isn't guaranteed?)

Second, some people really do just enjoy thinking about law that much. I can't pretend to understand such people, but apparently they exist. And if you're one of those people, you probably have a much better shot at being happy in law school and as a lawyer. So try reading a law review article that sounds interesting; many are available for free online. But don't just skim the article — actually read it. If you find it thought-provoking and inspiring, go forth to law school! But if not, think a little harder about how much you really like law. Because you will be expected to think about it a *lot.*

Clinicals & practical classes

Earlier, I mentioned clinical and practical classes. So what are they? Well, besides traditional lectures and seminars, there are skills-based classes (what I'm referring to as "practical classes") where you're actually *doing* something, not just engaging in academic debates. Examples of practical classes at Harvard include Trial Advocacy Workshop and Negotiation Workshop.

The first — and really, only — time I felt that I had made the right decision in going to law school was when I did Trial Advocacy Workshop my 2L year. TAW was basically Mock Trial for law students, and I'm not gonna lie, I rocked it pretty hard. But later, once I was actually practicing, I realized my folly: unless I wanted to practice criminal law (which I didn't), TAW was nothing like practicing law.

Allow me to explain. Broadly speaking, there are two types of law: civil and criminal. The basic difference is that civil law involves money while criminal law involves potential time in prison. (It gets a bit muddier with white-collar crime, but that's the general idea.) And because of the nature of the conduct that tends to be punished with prison versus fines, as well as differences in procedural safeguards, criminal cases go to court a lot more often.

In contrast, if you end up doing civil litigation, there's generally very little trial work.[19] And if you end up at a place

---

[19] I explain more about the difference between trial practice and litigation in Chapter 9 (Types of Practice in Biglaw). For now, all you need to know is that trials are the stuff of *Law & Order* and Mock Trial, and litigation involves writing a lot of documents either trying to get information or arguing why you should win on various disputes (because there are millions of small disputes that come up between filing a complaint and getting a decision on the ultimate issues in the case, if you even get that far).

that focuses on civil trial work — that is, being in court — it's not actually that fun (at least in my opinion), and mostly a lot of work. There's also a certain type of personality that gravitates towards trial work, and it's exactly the type you'd expect: loud and brash and in your face. Blech.

If you end up in criminal law, sure, it's interesting and less procedurally ridiculous, but it's one thing when you're dealing with other students like in TAW or Mock Trial, and another thing entirely when you're actually dealing with someone who has been accused of committing a serious crime. Some people can handle it, but I'm not one of those people. Are you?

But I digress. In addition to practical classes, there are clinicals, where you can basically practice law as a student and get class credit for it. Most, if not all, law schools have clinics, though the number and range will vary. (And as noted earlier, law schools also have extracurricular organizations to the same effect, except without the credit.)

So in my continuing effort to try to see what real law was like, I did a clinical at Harvard's Berkman Center for Internet and Society. That was my other favorite part of law school, at least of the stuff that was law-related. The people in the clinical were awesome and laid-back, and I got to work on cool technology-related stuff. I was finally doing something real, interesting, and for a good cause.

You might be wondering why I didn't do something related to that after law school, instead of going to a firm. Remember, I went to law school during the Great Recession: I took the first job I was offered. Other people in my year who were way more dedicated to public interest managed to scrounge up a fellowship for a year or two, but then were forced into the private sector as soon as their funding ran out.

But If I'm being honest, a lack of job opportunities isn't the whole story. At the end of the day, it came down to the money. Jobs at nonprofits pay next to nothing, and I had loans sky-high. I was also worried that I wasn't enough of a "believer," and that I wouldn't be able to grasp the technological knowledge necessary, since I was already struggling to understand tech law articles.

So in the end, it was simply fear that kept me from applying for those jobs: fear of not being able to make ends meet, fear of being ideologically inadequate, and fear of being intellectually inadequate. Don't get me wrong, I was afraid to go to a law firm too, but: (a) at least I wouldn't have to worry about money, and (b) it was what you're "supposed" to do right out of law school. Between my ingrained fear of money issues and the subtle pressures of law school that funneled me down that path, my ending up at a firm was inevitable.

I'm telling you all this for two reasons. First, law school sets you on a particular path, and it is incredibly difficult to deviate from that path. It's like trying to walk down a crowded up escalator: you can do it, but it's way more effort than just standing there, and you have to fight against the crowd. Second, what you enjoy doing in law school might not necessarily be something you can do or want to do once you leave. That's one of many reasons why it's important to have a deep understanding of why you want to go to law school.

Summer internships

"What about summer internships?" you ask. "Aren't those supposed to be real-world legal experiences too?"

Yes and no. Generally, your 1L summer internship is supposed to your "fun" summer, where you work at a place you're actually interested in (usually without pay), and then you work at a law firm your 2L year.

But if you go to a low-ranked school,[20] you're lucky to get anything. This is not me being a Harvard jerk; this is just the sad reality of the legal profession. Even if you're willing to work for free, there's only so much work to go around, and unless you have an inside connection, you can't get your foot

---

[20] In Chapter 15 (If You Still Want to Go to Law School), I'll talk in more detail about law school ranking.

in the door without law school name recognition. For example, most, if not all, of my fellow interns at the DOJ went to law schools ranked in the top 15 by U.S. News. And I was in the Tax and Antitrust Divisions — imagine how much more competitive a "sexier" division like Civil Rights is!

As far as 2L summer goes, I should note that I couldn't get a law firm gig like you're "supposed" to do. That's partly because I was under the misapprehension that I wanted to do corporate (transactional) law, which is not a great thing to say when there is no corporate work because of a massive economic recession. Here's another opportunity to learn from my mistake: the economy doesn't just impact how many jobs are available, but what *kinds* of jobs are available.

But once I was working at a firm after law school, I had the opportunity to observe summer interns for a few years, and here's what I saw: you do make a *ton* of money interning at a big law firm — around $30,000 — but it drains your life force. Summer internships at law firms give "work hard, play hard" a whole new meaning. You're constantly being taken out to fancy restaurants and fun events, and you're expected to attend all of them. You're also expected to do actual work, which meant that on several occasions, I saw summer interns staying later than the actual associates. By the end of the summer, all the interns look exhausted and have gained 20 pounds.

In contrast, I interned at the DOJ both summers in law school. There was no wining and dining, but I worked 9 to 5, except for when I got to travel for a trial. Not a bad gig. I don't think any government agency pays you if you're a 1L, and many are moving towards not paying you even as a 2L. But you can often get funding through your school, or at least get class credit. It's not ideal, but you'll get work experience, which is what internships are all about.

Regardless of where you intern, the type of work you do varies based on what's available at the moment (I'll talk more about how problematic this can be when we get to Part III — The Reality of Being a Lawyer). But generally, it will be some form of legal writing and research. If you're at a litigation-oriented place, you'll probably be researching the case law on some issue and writing a memo on what you find, and maybe drafting a motion or two if your work is good. If you're doing more transactional work, which is the other major type of legal practice, you might be researching public corporate documents or a statute that could affect a particular transaction, again drafting a memo on your findings (legal interns draft a lot of memos).

In terms of employment after law school, if you're lucky enough to land a law firm internship for your 2L summer, you usually get an offer to work there after graduation (unless you got too drunk at the intern picnic or the economy crashes). But the rest of the legal world hires based on need and budget, so while you're expected to do summer internships during law school, they don't mean much in terms of employment after graduation.

In short, law school doesn't do a great job of preparing you for legal practice, either through teaching you real-world skills or by helping you secure employment. While you'd still have to fend for yourself if you *didn't* go to law school, you wouldn't have the debt. Speaking of which...

Chapter 6: Dollars and Sense

It's time to talk about the financial burden of law school. You probably already know how much it costs (and if you don't, you're *really* not ready for law school), but there are still a few things worth discussing.

Merit scholarships

First, many merit scholarships require you to be in the top x percent of your class, or to keep your GPA above a certain level, in order to maintain your scholarship. As I mentioned in the introduction, this is really hard. If you're anything like me, you were told at every school transition point, "Ooh, things are going to get harder next year!", only to find out that that wasn't really the case. Trust me, with law school, it *will* be the case. This is in large part because law school is very different from all the school you've done before. (Yes, even if you've taken law-related classes.)

The point of law school isn't to educate you; it's to train you. And while you likely have some general aptitude for learning, law school focuses on developing a very narrow set of skills that you may or may not be good at. Before law school, I had always loved school and been at the top of my class. But law school was different. I didn't like the coursework, and I just wasn't good at "thinking like a lawyer" (despite having taken law-related classes in college). So definitely don't assume that you'll be good at law school just because you were good at college.

The second thing about merit scholarships is that if you get one, it might be a sign that you should set your sights higher. After all, law schools don't give out merit scholarships to their middling applicants. And even if you dominate at your lower-tier school, potential employers may not take the time to figure that out when they see that low-ranked school on your resume.

The law's a snob, remember? For college, it doesn't matter too much where you go as long as it's relatively decent. But for law school, the "name brand" matters a lot when you're looking for a job. So while you might be able to graduate debt-free with a merit scholarship, that won't matter a whole lot if your degree is useless in the job market.

Dropping out vs. not going at all

I've already talked about how I wanted to drop out of law school but ended up staying despite hating it. Dropping out is harder than just not going in the first place, because by that point: (a) you've already started accumulating significant debt; (b) you're probably used to achieving what you set out to do, which being a "dropout" is psychologically incompatible with; and (c) now that you're on an established path, it feels safer to stay on it than wander off into the unknown.

If you're reading this book, hopefully you haven't started down that path yet. And if I've convinced you to think twice about law school, I urge you to take as much time as you need to think it through *before* you commit. Dropping out is way more difficult and expensive than not going in the first place.

There's a term in economics called "opportunity cost." It refers to the potential benefits you lose when you pursue a certain course of action instead of a mutually exclusive alternative. As an example, when you go to college, the opportunity cost is the money plus interest you could have earned if you had started working full-time straight after high school. In this case, the point is that you can't get back the years that you'd be at law school — let alone the money that you'd spend to be there.

Opportunity costs are inevitable, since you will always face mutually exclusive alternatives with limited resources. Do I buy lunch or eat the bland leftovers from yesterday's dinner? Do I go away for the weekend with my friends or spend it cleaning my filthy apartment? Do I accept the job offer where I liked the people best or the one that's offering me a lot more money?

Ideally, you'd choose the path that produces the greatest overall benefit after accounting for opportunity costs — keeping in mind that psychological and other intangible effects, not just money, should be taken into account.

As I mentioned before, law school focuses on a narrow set of skills, and the time you spend developing those skills is time you're not spending on broader business and life skills. So if you decide after law school that you don't want to practice law, you'll be at a disadvantage compared to the folks who have already spent time honing those skills in the greater business world.[21] Law school is also ridiculously hard and draining, and the effect of that doesn't disappear when you graduate.

In short, the money, time, and energy you'd spend on law school is money, time, and energy that you can never get back. So make sure you spend it wisely. If you're not 100% sure you want to go to law school — and I mean 100% sure, not 99% — you're not ready to pay the cost.

Designing your lives. It's worth spending a little time thinking seriously about what you would do if you didn't go to law school. In the excellent book *Designing Your Life*, Bill Burnett and Dave Evans recommend coming up with three

---

[21] Take a look at Lisa's story in Chapter 3 (What Is a JD Good For?) for more on this.

different visions for the next five years of your life.[22] (Let's assume it's the five years after college, if you still have a few years of undergrad left.)

The first version is where you go to law school. But your other two alternatives should be substantially different, not just variations on a law-related theme. For version two, imagine everyone in the world got together and decided that lawyers and politicians weren't worth all the trouble they caused, so all the law schools were shut down and people figured out how to govern themselves. What would you do then?

Finally, version three is what you would do if money, image, and logistics were no object. Don't worry if it sounds silly or impracticable — that's the whole point!

Here's what my three imagined futures might have looked like after undergrad: In version #1, I'd go to law school, then go to DOJ Civil Rights or the ACLU. In version #2, I'd go to grad school for a Ph.D. in Philosophy. (If you're also considering grad school, please, please, please look into

---

[22] Bill Burnett and Dave Evans, *Designing Your Life* (New York: Alfred A. Knopf, 2016), 90-97. I've only described a lite version of the exercise here, so I highly recommend that you check the book out!

Hat tip to Dr. Kathryne Young, author of *How to Be Sort of Happy in Law School*, for suggesting this exercise, and to Nathan Elton for letting me steal his copy of *Designing Your Life*.

employment prospects. Because it is not pretty, especially outside of STEM.) In version #3, I'd move to New York and work as an editorial assistant at a big trade publisher like Random House.

There's no one right path for you to take. So use this opportunity to explore your potential. What makes you happy? What excites you (but maybe also terrifies you)? Where can you make a unique contribution?

Don't limit yourself. After all, you've got your whole life in front of you.

The psychological effect of debt

Having loads of debt — even the "good" kind, like student loans — has a crippling psychological effect. A 2013 study from Northwestern University surveying over 15,000 young adults ages 24 to 32 found that having a high debt-to-asset ratio "was associated with higher perceived stress and depression and worse self-reported general health, even when accounting for life-course health and economic conditions and other indices of current socioeconomic position."[23] Another 2013 study concluded that "student

---

[23] Elizabeth Sweet, Arijit Nandi, Emma K. Adam, and Thomas W. McDade, "The High Price of Debt: Household Financial Debt and Its Impact on Mental and Physical Health," *Social Science & Medicine* 91 (August 2013): 98.

loans are associated with poorer psychological functioning."[24]

In other words, if law school itself doesn't cause stress and depression for you, the debt it causes just might. So it's not surprising that after law school, people feel obligated to go to big law firms to start paying off that debt.

In my case, I went to a big law firm because I graduated in the midst of the Great Recession, and the law firm offer was the first job I got. I didn't have any undergraduate loans thanks to a merit scholarship, but aside from a few hundred dollars in need-based grants, I graduated with the full load of law school debt.

It took me five years of wearing "golden handcuffs" to pay off my loans. (Wearing "golden handcuffs" means that you're in a job that pays well — which, in turn, helps you pay off your loans — but you hate it.) And while five years might not sound terrible, there were many times during my biglaw career when I didn't know how I was going to get through the week or month, let alone the year. Even now, having safely escaped biglaw, I still rue those five years of my life I'll never get back. It's too easy to forget that life is finite.

---

[24] Katrina M. Walsemann, Gilbert C. Gee, and Danielle Gentile, "Sick of Our Loans: Student Borrowing and the Mental Health of Young Adults in the United States," *Social Science & Medicine* 124 (January 2015): 91.

That's not just a cliché: Studies have shown that we have a mental disconnect between our present self and our future self. It's a bit like we think someone else magically takes over our lives before we "reach" the future.

For example, in one study, students were asked to drink a disgusting mixture of ketchup and soy sauce for "scientific research." They could choose how much they drank, though they were told that the more they drank, the more helpful it would be to the researchers. Some were told that they would have to drink it in a few minutes; others, not for another semester. The students who believed they didn't have to do it until the following semester signed up to drink more than *twice as much* of the gross stuff as the students who had to do it immediately.[25] When the effects of our actions seem far away, it's easy to put off thinking about them.

On the other hand, when we feel like our we have a more immediate connection with the future, we grasp better how much the present contributes to what happens in the future. For instance, in another study, some participants looked at a computer-generated aged version of themselves that mirrored their actions, while others just looked in a real mirror. Both groups were then asked to allocate a

---

[25] Kelly McGonigal, *The Willpower Instinct: How Self-Control Works, Why It Matters, and What You Can Do to Get More of It* (New York: Avery, 2012), 172-73.

hypothetical budget of $1,000 among different categories, including present expenses, splurges, and retirement. The participants who interacted with their "future selves" put twice as much money in retirement as those who did not[26].

What does this have to do with law school? Well, we're willing to commit to painful things in the future because our brain doesn't quite comprehend that we're the ones who are going to have to suffer later. And for most people, law school is a painful thing.

But there are ways to see your future self as *you*, so that you're more apt to make choices you'll be happy with later, rather than whatever is easiest now. And in Chapter 12 (Look Inward First), I'll discuss how to do that.

---

[26] McGonigal, 176-78.

Part Three:

The Reality of Being a Lawyer

Chapter 7: The Big Picture

Before I delve into what practicing law looks like on a daily basis, let's talk about what makes people stay or leave.

From school to practice

Several of the people I interviewed expressed disappointment with the disparity between law school and law practice. For example, Will Meyerhofer, the lawyer-turned-psychotherapist, says, "I was terrific law student, but the actual practice of law was never my thing. I'm not an introvert, I hate details, I hate arguing and being adversarial, and I'm not all that interested in Wall Street or finance or money in general."

Most biglaw work revolves around money in one way or another. In addition to clients paying the firm an obscene amount of money — leading to increased pressure to do everything perfectly — the matters themselves frequently involve corporate finance, whether it's securities litigation, bankruptcy litigation, or a good old-fashioned merger. And if you're not interested in that, it can be boring and frustrating as hell. (Fun fact: Working at a law firm is where I first discovered that something can be boring *and* difficult at the same time.)

To other folks, legal practice itself is the problem. Lisa, who left law to work in Silicon Valley, says that she "loved law school, but the problem is that the practice of law is the practice — it's just doing the same thing over and over. It's stifling..." She believes that "law school has room for creativity, but the practice of law doesn't."

It's the nature of the beast: there's a process you have to follow for each case. The facts vary, but the process doesn't. Granted, that's more true for litigation than corporate, since litigation has actual rules while corporate work relies primarily on negotiation. But the basic goal is the same — get the client what they want — and the basic tools are the same.

To that end, don't settle for a practice area that you're not *actively excited* about. Not hating a practice area is not the same thing as actually liking it. It'll take longer for you to notice, but you'll wind up just as unhappy. Trust me.

Julie, a partner at a public interest firm, agrees that liking interesting legal questions, or law generally, isn't enough if you don't care about the substance of what you're doing. "Law school is a smorgasbord of trying different things, but working isn't like that. You have to wake up every day and actually go to work." So, she concludes, "[u]nless you find what motivates you, you're going to get stuck."

No acting, just reacting

There's not much room for big-picture creativity in law. Casey notes that a lot of his Leave Law Behind clients are "litigators who leave because they want something collaborative, they want to work on a team, they want to create something." For his own part, Casey found law "very reactive," where he "was always the bad guy, telling someone they couldn't do something."

Lawyers don't create anything original; they just react to whatever they're given. Sure, you could argue that lawyers "create" arguments and case strategies and written work like briefs and memos, but I mean "create" in the sense of contributing something altogether new to the world. As Casey said, being a lawyer is reactive — you never get to *proactively* contribute. The late Supreme Court Justice Antonin Scalia agreed, saying in a 2009 interview with C-SPAN:[27]

> [T]here'd be a, you know, a ... public defender from Podunk, you know, and this woman is really brilliant, you know. Why isn't she out

---

[27] Elie Mystal, "Justice Antonin Scalia Says Some of the Best Minds May Be Wasted on Law," *Above the Law,* October 1, 2009, https://abovethelaw.com/2009/10/justice-antonin-scalia-says-some -of-the-best-minds-may-be-wasted-on-law/.

inventing the automobile or, you know, doing something productive for this society?

... [L]awyers, after all, don't produce anything. They enable other people to produce and to go on with their lives efficiently and in an atmosphere of freedom. That's important, but it doesn't put food on the table and there have to be other people who are doing that. And I worry that we are devoting too many of our very best minds to this enterprise.

Compare that to Karen, a nonprofit-lawyer-turned-software-engineer, who says that her new career gives her "the chance to fix tangible problems on a daily basis in a way I always hoped legal practice would allow."

No room for innovation

Relatedly, there's not a whole lot of room for innovation. As I discussed in the Prologue, in law you have to do things as they were done before, almost by definition. A system built on precedents means that all you can do is your best with whatever is there. In addition, there are rules at every level, and if you break them, you lose. Often literally.

Lisa remarked on this difference, saying, "My current job is so different from law. Silicon Valley's focus is on execution and outcome, whereas in law, the focus is on process."

In a way, law can't help being process-based. In litigation at least, you have so little control over whether you win. I've known a judge to deny a motion to dismiss on grounds that didn't make any sense (because under that reasoning, a motion to dismiss could literally never be granted); another judge who was going to rule one way in a major case but was convinced by his clerk to rule otherwise; and a criminal case that should clearly have ended in a conviction wind up with a hung jury instead, due to the "holiday season" phenomenon. There's no such thing as a sure thing. And in both litigation and corporate practice, there's always the opposing side that wants the opposite of whatever you want and will fight you to get it.

So the practice of law has to focus on process rather than outcome, because you don't have control over the ultimate outcome. Yes, you can negotiate and advocate zealously and so forth, but at the end of the day, you're stuck with whatever the judge or jury decides or the other party agrees to. To put it another way, you can improve individual briefs and contracts, but you can't improve the *system*.

Opportunities are random

If you view outcome in terms of skills development, rather than as the outcome of any given matter, it doesn't look much better. For instance, at a big law firm, depending on what cases you get assigned to, you could be doing nothing but doc review for a year or two. Meanwhile, your friend, who started at the firm at the same time, is working on depositions and summary judgment briefs, because her case already finished e-discovery and is on an accelerated timetable.

And if you're interested in going into government, the types of cases you work on and the official positions you take in those cases may depend on the political administration, since they dictate the agenda. For instance, in the Antitrust Division of the Department of Justice, there tends to be less investigation of mergers and more criminal prosecutions when there's a Republican administration. As another example, I worked at the Federal Communications Commission (FCC) when Donald Trump was elected in 2016, and the attorneys in the FCC's Office of General Counsel suddenly had to stop prosecuting cases or else reverse their position overnight.

You also have no control over how long cases take. Ideally, cases would settle or otherwise be resolved quickly, but complex litigation can and does go on for years, and sometimes you just have obnoxious opposing counsel who drag their feet or file a million motions, or a judge who takes a long time to issue orders (since judges don't have any deadlines).

In short, it's basically luck of the draw, and it's not uncommon to hear stories of people who spent several years on cases they hated. At firms, once you establish relationships with partners, you at least have slightly more control over who you work with, which makes a difference. But even they can't control what comes through the door.

Hierarchy

Another reason for the lack of innovation is the rigid hierarchy. Why bother trying to think up new ways to do things when the regular stuff you do just gets changed more and more at every level anyway? It's especially frustrating when the changes aren't necessarily improvements. I remember one time a draft that I had written went up the chain and became more and more wordy and unrecognizable as everyone added their "edits," until one of the reviewing partners circled a sentence that had been particularly burdened by too many cooks in the metaphorical kitchen and wrote in big letters, "Guys, can't we write better than this??"

The other major downside is that everything you do has to be approved by someone. A friend of mine worked tirelessly to write and re-write a legal journal article at the behest of a high-ranking partner — which doesn't count toward billable hours, by the way — only to have it rejected by a firm committee because some clients in the industry might not have liked it. (Obviously it was in the gray area, or else the partner wouldn't have wanted the article written in the first place. But still.)

Hierarchy is basically code for playing it safe. After all, the ones calling the shots are the guys who stuck around long enough to accept and master telling people no and being the bad guy.

As discussed further in Chapter 10 (Life in Other Legal Environments), this is less of a problem in government. You get a seat at the table straightaway, if only because they're perpetually understaffed. However, while there are fewer layers to the hierarchy in government, it's still alive and well.

You have to love law

Many of the interviewees noted their love of law as a key reason why they're happy being lawyers. One biglaw attorney says, "I think what allows me to survive is love of the law. I see a lot of people leave the law in the early associate years because those years are really, really, hard, especially if you are trying to balance it with a family. I read somewhere that junior associate attorneys consistently rate as the unhappiest workers. You can't make it through those years without loving the law."

Julie, the partner at a public interest firm, agrees. "I love law," she says, "but I understand why some people don't like it. You have to have a weird personality to like it."

Similarly, another biglaw attorney, Allison, says of her time as a paralegal, "I enjoyed going to work all the time." She considers herself "fortunate" to have been at a law firm during the Great Recession, since, due to the staff shortage, she got to do "borderline lawyer work."

One trend I noticed among the lawyers who stayed in law is that many of them either are first-generation Americans or come from working-class families, where they were the first in their family to go to college, let alone law school. My theory is that these folks have different values from privileged brats like myself, and maybe also a keen knowledge of what they *don't* want their lives to be like, which allows them to enjoy — or at least be satisfied with — being lawyers.

Basically, if you don't love law with a burning passion, and you cringe at the thought of working long and tough hours on something you may not be passionate about, law school probably isn't for you.

Chapter 8: Working at a Big Law Firm

Since most kids from good law schools go to big law firms after graduation — and you should only go to law school if you can get into a good school[28] — this chapter covers some hard truths about biglaw life.

You're never off the clock

The general rule of thumb with law firms is that the "better" the firm, the more demanding it is, and the less tolerance it has for personal time. As one senior associate notes, "If you work in biglaw, you have to be on call all the time. Which is fine for one or two years when you're single. But think about when you want to have kids. Or a healthy relationship, for that matter."

Case in point: A few years ago, Above the Law, a well-known blog for lawyers, had a post about Quinn Emanuel, a top-tier trial litigation law firm. The junior associate there had failed to send out a fax because he had stopped checking his Blackberry[29] after business hours and thus didn't get the partner's request to send the fax. Why this was notable?

---

[28] I talked about this a bit in the Introduction, but it's also covered more extensively in Chapter 15 (If You Still Want to Go to Law School).

[29] Some of you may be too young to know what a Blackberry is, which I will try not to be bitter about. Long story short, a Blackberry was kind of like a smartphone for work, except that that it was dumb.

Because the incident caused the partner to send out the following email to the firm:

> You should check your emails early and often. That not only means when you are in the office, it also means after you leave the office as well. Unless you have very good reason not to (for example when you are asleep, in court or in a tunnel), you should be checking your emails every hour. One of the last things you should do before you retire for the night is to check your email. That is why we give you blackberries [sic].[30]

Let me tell you, I've checked my Blackberry right before I had intended to go to sleep. That is almost always a mistake. Think about it: You're getting tired and winding down for bed, but you check your email one last time just in case. And guess what? You have an email from a partner, asking you to look into some issue ASAP. Sure, you consider waiting until the morning to start working on it, but now you're awake because you're worrying about it. Congratulations, you're not going to sleep for another four hours.

Here's a secret I learned a while back: The lawyers who thrive at law firms are the ones who don't need sleep. For

---

[30] Elie Mystal, "Quinn Emanuel Believes in 'C.B.A.' (Check BlackBerry Always)," *Above the Law*, October 16, 2009, http://abovethelaw.com /2009/10/quinn-emanuel-believes-in-c-b-a-check-blackberry-always/.

instance, Allison, who's now a partner at a big law firm, knew she could handle the hours from her time working as a paralegal on a trial. (Unlike Mock Trial, real trials require working ridiculously hard on little or no sleep for the whole trial.) Indeed, she says, "Not only could I work the hours, it was the most fun I had." But, she admits, "I think I'm more the exception than the norm."

Whether it's because you're working with folks on the other side of the country, or you're about to go to trial, or you're just really busy, you need to be able to run on fumes. I just could not do that, especially for extended periods of time. Be honest with yourself about what you need, because life will suck otherwise.

I remember going to a career panel during law school, featuring partners and a senior associate from big law firms. When they were asked what issues they see with young associates, the senior associate immediately answered, "Entitlement." The other panelists agreed. In this case, entitlement seemed to mean not wanting to spend your life at the office or do menial work.

Now, menial work is unavoidable as a lawyer, but I question how much of wanting to enjoy your work and/or have a life outside of work is "entitlement," versus just having different priorities from older generations. Regardless, the fact of the matter is that law firms are paying you big bucks with the expectation that you will put in the time accordingly. Which is to say, they own you, or at least think they do.

Will Meyerhofer, the ex-lawyer turned therapist/blogger, has a great post where he riffs on this idea:[31]

> I lost track, at Sullivan & Cromwell, of how many times I was told, "What did you expect? Why do you think we pay you so much?" There was often no detectable prompt to trigger this statement; it was just something people said to me for the heck of it, as in:
>
> Me: "Nice weather we're having."
>
> Them: "What did you expect? Why do you think we pay you so much?"

As Will quips, "I think they were a bit self-conscious about keeping human slaves and this was a way for them to assuage said self-consciousness."[32]

During the Q&A portion of the career panel, I dared to raise a question about work/life balance, asking, "I've heard

---

[31] Will Meyerhofer, "Why You're So Unhappy," *The People's Therapist*, November 4, 2015, https://thepeoplestherapist.com/2015/11/04/why -youre-so-unhappy/.

[32] You should read the whole blog post, as it has a great discussion of the three "vitamins" you need to actually like your job, based on the Basic Psychological Needs Scale. (And really, you should just read anything Will writes.)

that it's important to draw boundaries early on so you don't burn out. What's the best way to do that?"

The panelist who answered, a partner at a big law firm in New York City, said that we weren't allowed to have boundaries. The actual words she used are hazy, but I vividly remember the way she said "boundaries" with scorn and contempt dripping from her voice.

At a different point in the discussion, the same panelist also said that you should always do everything perfectly and ahead of time. I made a note of her name and law firm so I could make sure to never, ever go there. But I think her sentiment is shared by most biglaw partners — she was just more brazen than most in saying it.

No room for error

That's another thing: there's no tolerance for mistakes, especially in high-pressure situations. But that's exactly when a lot of folks, including myself, tend to make the most mistakes. And unfortunately, there are a lot of high-pressure situations at big law firms. A high-pressure situation can be anything from a deal closing or filing deadline (since people are almost always editing and revising documents until the last minute), to an entire case where everything is stressful all the time, whether because the case is high stakes or because the partner is mean, disorganized, or otherwise terrible.

Which brings me to another downside of the rigid hierarchal structure at big law firms: everyone is considered responsible for the work of the people below them. So you better believe they're either going to micromanage your ass or chew you out if you do anything wrong. Since "wrong" can also mean "not how they would have done it," it's especially fun when you're working for multiple partners on a project who have different ideas on how things should be done and don't communicate with each other. Not that I'm speaking from experience or anything. (I totally am.)

Oh, the hell of multiple bosses. If I had a dollar for every time I got emails from different partners on the same night saying that they needed something "first thing" in the morning, I'd have been able to pay off my student loans way faster. Everyone thinks their project is the most important. They don't care what else you're working on as long as you put their project first.

Okay, that might not be entirely fair — in most cases, they just don't know what else you're working on — but they do expect you to be at their beck-and-call once you're on their case. (Speaking of which, don't ever, ever, ever believe someone who asks you to join their project and promises that your involvement in a case will be limited. That's the trick they pull when you say you're too busy but they're still trying to get you to join the case. It's a lie.)

And since legal matters are by nature unpredictable, due to too many moving parts and too much siloing of information, that means they can and will expect you to drop everything when they call you out of the blue, regardless of whether you're already jammed on something else. This screws you over in at least two ways. First, it screws you over on your billable hours, because you won't know whether to pick something else up, so you could take on too little or too much (more about this in the next section). Second, it screws you over in terms of your well-being, since there's nothing to prevent two cases from going crazy at once. And they do.

Now, you may be thinking, "Doesn't a lot of this applies to *any* job, legal or otherwise?" It's true, you certainly don't have to be a lawyer to work with demanding clients or a boss that micromanages you, or to be confronted with an unexpected emergency on a big project. But because there's so much money at stake — both in terms of how much clients are paying your firm and how much they stand to lose — biglaw lawyers and their clients tend to get a little extra crazy.

Billable hours

Billable hours refers to the time you spend doing work that can be billed to a client. Seems reasonable enough, especially considering that other types of businesses, like consulting and accounting, use billable hours as well. But somehow law firms have twisted it into a rat race that's impossible to win.

It's a catch-22: If you're billing a lot, you're not sleeping. But if you're *not* billing a lot, you're worried about getting fired. It's just another way in which law firms make you feel stressed out *all the time*. I don't know why billable hours are so uniquely terrible in the legal profession, but they are.

If you think I'm exaggerating, just google "the tyranny of the billable hour." Because that's a thing.[33] Lisa says that when she was at a big law firm, "I didn't feel like it mattered if I did a great job or just an okay job, as long as I billed a certain number of hours. At my new job in Silicon Valley, I feel empowered to *do* stuff."

---

[33] For an overview of how the billable hour has been used and abused in the U.S. legal industry, including how expectations went from 1,300 hours in 1958 to over 2,000 now, check out Stuart L. Pardau, "Bill, Baby, Bill: How the Billable Hour Emerged as the Primary Method of Attorney Fee Generation and Why Early Reports of Its Demise May Be Greatly Exaggerated," *Idaho Law Review* 50, no. 1 (2013).

Moreover, not all time spent working is billable. Even beyond necessities like going to the bathroom, there are everyday administrative tasks, such as entering your timesheet, that aren't billable. Other examples of non-billable work include client development (that is, efforts to get new clients), continuing legal education (required by most state bars), and writing articles. In fact, a 2021 study by a legal technology company determined that on average, **only about 31% of a lawyer's time, or 2.5 hours in an 8-hour day, is spent on billable work.**[34]

And don't be fooled by firms that say they don't have a minimum billable-hour requirement. They're not promoting work-life balance. Quite the opposite, in fact: there's no explicit minimum billable-hour requirement because they want you to get paranoid and competitive and work extra hard because you're worried you might be falling behind, since you have no idea what other people are billing. And if you choose to stay out of the competition, you're at risk for being fired.

Similarly, don't be fooled by firms claiming that you can count an unlimited number of pro bono hours towards your billables. ("Pro bono" refers to the free public interest work that you're theoretically encouraged to do.) I don't care how

---

[34] *2021 Legal Trends Report* (Clio, 2021): 36, https://www.clio.com/wp-content/uploads/2021/08/2021-Legal-Trends-Report-Oct-26.pdf.

much those firms protest that they don't distinguish between billable and pro bono on your hours summary, because they absolutely do differentiate, even if the pro bono is not explicitly delineated on whatever form the partners see about your hours. Did I mention lack of transparency is also a big problem at law firms?

And don't get too excited by firms that offer unlimited vacation. It's kind of the inverse of not having a minimum billable-hour requirement: they're hoping that by not giving you a specified amount of time off, you won't take any. Plus, you'll only feel comfortable taking time off if you're not too busy at work. Which, per the billable-hour catch-22, either you are super busy, or you're freaking out about not being busy. Either way, you'll most likely end up working while on vacation anyway.

Figure it out yourself

Some law firms also claim to have a "free market" system, in which you're responsible for managing your own work flow, as opposed to a formal assignment system. To the extent it works, it's a mixed blessing: you can choose your own work, but on the other hand, you have to find your own work.

There's also a huge extent to which it's not a free market at all. For instance, it's "understood" that when certain partners ask you to work on matters, you do it. Period. You'll know which partners they are, because they are the ones that everyone knows. They are the Institutions. Even if you think your plate is already full, if they're coming to you (and you don't otherwise have a relationship with them), that means they think you have time. It also means that it's likely to be a high-profile, high-pressure case, since those are the only cases that Institutions work on.

At the same time, you have to look out for yourself, because no one else will. But sometimes it's hard to even know *how* to look out for yourself. Do you turn down a new project because one of your current projects may get really busy in a few weeks (but also might not)? Do you take on a pro bono project that seems awesome but will likely take up a lot of your time (thus taking away time from billable matters and/or sleep)? What about the partner you've been dying to work for who finally asks you to join a case, but you're already billing more than you can handle? And we won't even talk about your personal life (or should I say, lack thereof).

No human contact

Even for a hardcore introvert like myself, working at a law firm was lonely. I'd be stuck at my desk all day, doing some research and/or writing assignment, only seeing other people for a couple of minutes out of my day when I went to the bathroom or did a quick circuit around the halls to get some feeling back into my legs. Otherwise, everyone else was either similarly locked in their office or traveling for work.

I resorted to baking to try to lure people to my office so I'd actually have some human contact. I also learned the hard way that you can only schedule lunch with one other person, or it will never happen. Even then, it will take at least a month to find a time when both of you are free. And the odds are good that it will end up being a quick coffee instead of lunch, because that's all you have time for.

Think I'm exaggerating? In between my two years at the first law firm I worked at, I left for a year to clerk for a federal judge. When I came back, several people *didn't realize that I had left*. They thought I had just been really busy. For a year.

State of emergency

So what is working at a law firm like day-to-day? The rote response is, "There is no typical day." But that's not really helpful, is it? (And yet, lawyers never stop giving that answer.) Yes, your actual tasks will probably vary. But there's still a disturbing pattern to your days. Or rather, two patterns. The first pattern consists of you working on something fairly mundane, with nothing else to do, for a long period of time, until you want to scream. Examples include long-term doc review projects (more on doc review in the next chapter) and extensive research memos on boring topics.

The second pattern involves you planning what you're going to accomplish that day, and then doing none of it because people keep interrupting you to make you do other things. A common variation of this pattern is where you're toiling away on a time-sensitive project for one case when a partner from a different case that you haven't worked on for months calls and tells you to do something immediately because that case is suddenly exploding. (And somehow those calls never, ever come when you're in pattern #1.)

You'll often hear the term "fire drill" bandied about in such situations. Fire drills refer to when you suddenly and unexpectedly have to get a lot of work done very, very quickly. It's incredibly high-stress, all the more so because you didn't see it coming. But despite being a phrase used constantly at law firms, everyone seems to forget that the nature of a fire drill is that it's a *drill*, not an actual life-or-death situation.

Which brings me to a crucial point that most people seem to forget once they're at a firm: *Nothing law firms do is that important.* In fact, some would argue that it matters only insofar as the law firms are often representing companies that the general public view as corrupt and immoral, which is to say that it only matters in a bad way. Yes, there's pro bono work and the like, but let's face it, that's not the law firm's bread and butter.

I remember getting a dramatic email from a senior partner about a high-profile case the firm had just taken on, asking me to join the case. After giving an overview of the case, he asked, "Will you help our client in its time of need?"

The client in question was a Fortune 500 company against whom a personal injury class action had been brought. It was clear that the company had engaged in wrongdoing; it was just a question of limiting the liability. Yet the partner felt that the company was somehow being victimized. Moral of the story: You need to binge-drink the Kool-Aid to make partner.

Relatedly, it's not unusual to hear partners treat cases like battles. For instance, I remember a team meeting for a different case where another partner kept saying that the client company "is fighting a war on multiple fronts," "being attacked on all sides," "surrounded by enemies," and the like. And since it's "war," they're more than willing to resort to tactics like dumping a bunch of documents on the other side right before Christmas, or filing a motion so that they'll have to respond right after a holiday, thus ruining said holiday.

But war is about life and death. Law isn't, at least in the vast majority of cases. And in civil litigation, which is most of what law firms do, it's only ever about who pays. But it's too easy to lose sight of that when you're in the thick of it.

Getting fired (and hired)

As you've probably gathered at this point, succeeding at a law firm is basically an endurance test. So what happens if you run out of steam?

Most law firms are based on a pyramid structure, with lots of associates at the bottom and a small number of partners at the top. But that's only sustainable if associates get sloughed off as they try to climb the ladder to potential partnership. Firms have helpfully standardized the process by doing it during annual reviews.

So each year at your review, you either get promoted or asked to leave. Sometimes you'll be put on probation for a few months so you can get your act together before they decide whether to promote or fire you. Most people get asked to leave when they're trying to make the jump from associate to partner, but several still get cast off along the way. (Of course, many people also leave voluntarily, since working at a biglaw firm is no picnic.)

If you get asked to leave your biglaw firm, the typical move is to go to another biglaw firm, but in the next tier down. Remember, everything has a ranking in law: when you're fresh out of law school, you generally try to go to the most prestigious law firm you can, and then you can work your way down from there. Plus, smaller firms generally want more experienced people (since they have less bandwidth and money for training), and the government has a limited number of entry-level legal positions.

The standardization of the biglaw process is how law students end up at firms in the first place: they go to on-campus interviewing (OCI), which is designed to make it easier to get a job. While the idea is nice, OCI is 99% biglaw firms. Biglaw firms also tend to hire well before anyone else, so when you get an offer and you don't know when or if you'll get another one (not to mention that paycheck), it makes sense to accept it. And that's how they get you.

Mental health, revisited

Will Meyerhofer was fired from his top-tier law firm about two years after graduating law school. People expected Will to follow the usual path of going to a second-tier law firm. "But," Will says, "I was so miserable at law — it felt so utterly wrong for me — that the very thought of returning to a law firm gave me anxiety attacks."

Instead, he worked as a mid-level marketing exec at a dot com before ultimately deciding to become a psychotherapist. Now Will has his own practice — he specializes in counseling lawyers, because there's enough unhappy lawyers to do that — and a thriving blogging presence as the People's Therapist.

After getting fired from my own top-tier law firm, I had a similar reaction to Will. While I did go to a second-tier law firm (one that had a reputation for being kinder and gentler), I began getting migraines every Monday morning like clockwork. I think once my body realized that I was just doing a different version of the same old shit, it rebelled.

Here, I have to say a word in praise of the second firm, because it had an incredibly progressive program — especially by biglaw standards — where you could, for *any* reason, reduce your billable hour target by a certain percentage in exchange for a corresponding reduction in pay. While I had intended to wait a year before requesting it, I didn't last that long. By a lot. Barely two months after I started at the firm, I ended up sobbing in the office of the person who ran the program. And to their credit, when I had to tell the partners and senior associates that I worked for about my reduced hours, no one questioned it.

But unfortunately, biglaw is still biglaw. While my reduction in hours helped, it wasn't enough. Yes, my hours were reduced, but I still had little control over when I did them. Why? Because lawyering is about reacting, and you never know when something is going to come up that you need to react to.

It ain't all about the money

It's very, very easy, almost astonishingly so, to get used to the obscene biglaw salary. That's especially true if this is your first full-time job, since you have nothing to compare it to. And let's be honest: getting a six-figure salary makes you feel valued. After all, you must be pretty special to make that kind of money, right?

All of that makes it harder to quit when you realize you're slowly dying. So you convince yourself that you can stick it out a little longer because it sure would be nice to have some savings in the bank, and it's not like there are a lot of jobs where you can make that much right out of school.

By that point, you've moved to an expensive city, and of course you want to live in a decent neighborhood, and you need to splurge once in a while since you're working so hard, and don't forget those student loans that you need to pay off. Before you know it, you're spending almost all of your ridiculously high salary, which suddenly doesn't seem so ridiculously high as it did before.

Sonja Lyubomirsky, author of *The How of Happiness,* points to a study that surveyed people over 36 years on how much money they believed was needed by a family of four to "get along."[35] As the study participants made more money, their estimate of how much money was "needed" for that hypothetical family rose too. According to Lyubomirsky, "the estimate for 'get along' income increased almost exactly to the same degree as did actual income, suggesting that the more you have, the more you think you 'need.'"[36]

You do *not* want to get stuck thinking that you need six figures to get by. Trust me.

Being in the club

The one perk, aside from the money, is that you get to be "in the club." You can throw around phrases like "motion to compel" and "third-party subpoena" and actually know what they mean and therefore feel superior to other people who don't.

There's certainly no shame in wanting to be an expert. Just make sure that law is what you want to be an expert in. Imagine talking about law *all day*. I don't mean that figuratively — I want you to really imagine what it'd be like to spend 95% of your day talking about law, instead of sports or movies or whatever you talk about now. If the thought

---

[35] Sonja Lyubomirsky, *The How of Happiness: A New Approach to Getting the Life You Want* (New York: Penguin Books, 2007), 140.

[36] Lyubomirsky, 140.

doesn't bore you to tears, I give you my blessing to consider becoming a lawyer.

And yes, it's possible that your legal knowledge may come in handy in the real world. But remember what I said earlier: the better the law school, the less practical stuff you learn. Plus, the work you do at big law firms for big corporations has nothing to do with the law you'd need to know for your friends and family. I can't remember how many times a friend would ask me for advice about issues with their landlord or ex, and I'd have no idea what to tell them.

At the end of the day, if you're justifying going to law school because you think it might come in handy to know your way around the legal system even if you don't practice, remember that you could just hire a lawyer instead of plunging hundreds of thousands of dollars into debt. How much is the off-chance that you might learn something useful worth to you?

Chapter 9: Types of Practice in Biglaw

While I've given you the highlights (or rather, lowlights) of daily life at a firm, it's worth digging into the different types of practice a little further, since few college students — or even law students — know much about the nitty-gritty of practicing law. The traditional divide has been between litigation and corporate work, though regulatory work has also recently emerged as an alternative. (My own background is in litigation and regulatory work, so I'm relying on research and friends' accounts for my discussion of corporate work.) I'm not going to discuss all the individual practice areas like antitrust, bankruptcy, securities, intellectual property, etc., but this should give you a sense of the different overall types of legal practice.

Litigation

First, litigation is not the same as trial work. Litigation is the process of going through a lawsuit, and there's a helluva lot that happens before trial. Most big law firms focus the stuff *before* the trial,[37] which makes sense, since: (a) it can go

---

[37] The one exception I'm aware of is Quinn Emanuel, a big law firm that specializes in trial litigation and has the alpha personalities to match. A friend of mine who worked there — not an alpha, bless his heart — used to hide out in his car so he could finally get some sleep.

on for years before trial, and (b) only 2-3% of both civil and criminal cases even go to trial.[38]

Litigation is also unpredictable. You have no knowledge of or control over when the judge will rule on a motion, you have no knowledge of or control over when the other side will file motions, and you have only marginally more knowledge and control about when they will produce documents and witnesses. So you spend most of your time feeling powerless and in the dark. As one former litigator notes, "I was terrified that if I went on vacation for a week, an emergency would come up that I'd miss." And let me tell you, his fear was not unfounded.

So what happens between filing a lawsuit and trial? As a junior litigation associate, you will spend most of your time doing one of two things: research or discovery. If you're very good and very lucky, you'll get to do some writing as well

---

[38] John Barkai, Elizabeth Kent, and Pamela Martin. "A Profile of Settlement." *Court Review: The Journal of the American Judges Association* 42, no. 3 (December 2006): 34, http://aja.ncsc.dni.us /courtrv/cr42-3and4/CR42-3BarkaiKentMartin.pdf; John Gramlich, "Only 2% of Federal Criminal Defendants Go to Trial, and Most Who Do Are Found Guilty," *Pew Research Center,* June 11, 2019, https://www.pewresearch .org/fact-tank/2019/06/11/only-2-of-federal-criminal-defendants-go-to -trial-and-most-who-do-are-found-guilty/; "Report: Guilty Pleas on the Rise, Criminal Trials on the Decline," *Innocence Project,* August 7, 2018, https://www.innocenceproject.org/guilty-pleas-on-the-rise-criminal-trials -on-the-decline/.

(though it will be revised about a million times before it gets filed).

Research. As I discussed in Chapter 1, common law — which is what the U.S. has — is based on precedent, i.e., the cases that have come before. So if you go into litigation, you will spend a lot of time doing research on Westlaw or Lexis, hoping: (1) you will find a favorable case exactly on point, and (2) you will not miss the one damaging, obscure case, because opposing counsel will *always* find it. On top of that, the issues that you'll be asked to research will almost never be straightforward, even if the partner assures you that they should be.

Long story short, you can spend your entire life researching and still not be 100% confident that you didn't miss anything. And there's always more searches you can try, so you're never sure when you should hang up the towel.

Discovery. No one likes discovery, but it constitutes about 80% of civil litigation. So what is it, exactly?

Due to procedural safeguards, there shouldn't be surprises from either side in civil litigation. (In criminal cases, the prosecutor can't surprise the defense, but the defense can pretty much do whatever it wants, since the defendant is the one at risk of going to jail.) So all those movies where there's a personal injury suit and then it turns out the big bad law firm hid key documents? Yeah, not so much in real life.

There are legitimate lawyerly ways to try to keep documents away from opposing counsel or the jury, so lawyers who actually know what they're doing wouldn't bother with such risky tactics.

Anyway, the process that the parties engage in to avoid surprises is called discovery. There are two overall phases of discovery, fact discovery and expert discovery. In fact discovery, each side has to make a set of initial disclosures, including where relevant information is and who has it. After that comes written discovery, which comes in three forms: requests for admission, interrogatories, and document requests.

Requests for Admission. Requests for admission, or RFAs, are exactly what they sound like: you're asking the other party to admit that something is true. I haven't seen them used very often, probably because it's almost impossible to get a straight admission from a lawyer.

Interrogatories. Interrogatories are written questions sent by one party to another, which have to be answered under oath. Writing responses to interrogatories is probably one of the first opportunities for real legal writing experience that you'll get at a law firm, after research memos. You have to write objections to almost every interrogatory — as many objections as you can think of, since you never know which one the judge might uphold if it comes up in court — and then the substantive response. It's kinda fun for the first few, until you realize you have to do twenty more of them. Then it becomes less fun very quickly.

Once interrogatories have been exchanged and responded to, you meet and confer with opposing counsel to discuss the objections and try to reach compromises. Meet-and-confers are required under the rules whenever there's a discovery dispute. And if there's an objection, there's a dispute. So you have to go over each one with opposing counsel and argue about what information you're going to provide, if any. It's exactly as tediously painstaking as it sounds.

Document Requests. For the document requests, you have to meet and confer with the other side again, this time to decide on search terms and custodians. Before that happens, you'll have already collected documents from folks at your client's company with knowledge of the matter (the "custodians"). The bigger the company, the more documents it generates, so collecting hundreds of thousands, if not millions, of documents is on par for corporate litigation.

The next step is to hash out with the other side who the most important custodians are and what search terms you]re going to run on their documents. As you'd expect, the other side will always want more custodians and broader search terms from you, and the opposite for their own document production. In a medium-sized case I was on, just negotiating custodians and search terms took several conference calls over a couple of weeks. It was excruciating to sit there listening to the senior attorneys debate about whether to use an ampersand (&) or "within [n] words" to connect terms.

Doc Review. Then, of course, there's the process of actually reviewing the documents (the dreaded "doc review"). You have to review two sets of documents: the set that you're producing to the other side, and the set that they're producing to you. You're basically reviewing the documents to see if they're relevant, keeping an eye out for the occasional document that may be important or protected by privilege. Depending on how many documents there are, how complex and/or sensitive the documents are, how much time you have, and the client's preferences, you'll either have a team of associates at the firm doing the doc review, or you'll bring in contract attorneys (independent attorneys who do doc reviews on a per-project basis).

Doc review is one of those soul-sucking, no-win activities: you can't really "ace" it, but you can definitely screw it up. It requires careful attention to things that aren't interesting at all, like financial spreadsheets. Or 2-sentence emails where you have no idea what they're talking about and it probably doesn't matter but just in case you should try to figure it out, so now you have to look through your reference binder (where the attorneys in charge of the doc review have compiled instructions, key information, and names), flip through some more documents in case it's part of an email chain, and ask around — all for one document that may be completely irrelevant. On top of that, it's pretty much guaranteed that the database containing the documents will crash, probably several times in the middle of a particularly urgent review, and that everything will take way longer than you expected and budgeted for.

Dep Prep. Once written discovery is mostly done, you start preparing for depositions ("dep prep"). Part of the purpose of doc review is to get ready for depositions, both to prepare your own witnesses and to take the opposing witnesses' depositions. So what is a deposition? Well, as a further part of the process to avoid surprises, you get to question the other side's witnesses under oath *before* trial, with counsel for both sides and a court reporter present. (The judge isn't involved unless there's a serious issue, which is extremely rare, because no one wants to piss off the judge by calling them about something the attorneys should have been able to resolve themselves.)

In most cases, the deposition is just kind of just an exploratory mission to gather more information and get an idea of what the witness would say on the stand, and maybe try to get a few admissions, especially if you think they're unlikely to testify at trial, since the number of trial witnesses is usually limited. So when you're reviewing documents as part of dep prep, you're looking to see if there are any bad documents that you need to prepare your witnesses for, or helpful documents to use against the other side's witnesses.

For your own witnesses, you'll probably only get one, maybe two, prep sessions with them. After all, while lawyering may be your job, it's not theirs, so dealing with you is mostly seen as an inconvenience and distraction from their actual work. And since you won't have much time with them, half the battle is narrowing down the set of documents you want to ask them about. If you're lucky, you'll get to attend the dep prep with the witness and maybe even the actual deposition. But it's also entirely possible that you'll do all the work and not get to see any of it. Welcome to show biz, folks.

Experts. After depositions, you get into expert discovery. You'll have already found and retained experts to testify about how their expertise indicates that you should win. Specifically, you "help" them write expert reports to support your theory of the case. As a junior associate, you're likely to be tasked with finding an expert (which mostly involves a lot of Googling) and/or reviewing everything they've ever done to find anything that can be used to hurt your case (which also involves a lot of Googling).

But just because they're an expert doesn't mean they have to be an expert in anything *interesting*. For example, you'll usually have an economics expert regarding damages, which essentially boils down to just calculating monetary values for everything. And the other side will have their economic expert with his own calculation of damages, which will either be much higher or much lower depending on which side is the plaintiff or defendant. It's basically a battle of made-up numbers, and you have to argue about why your numbers are more right than their numbers.

Post-Discovery. Discovery takes months, if not years. Assuming the parties haven't settled during that time, you start preparing for trial. You — or rather, the partner — will meet with the judge to decide on a trial schedule (which also would have happened for discovery), setting dates for things like exchanging witness and exhibits lists, filing any pre-trial motions, and, of course, the actual trial. It's not unusual for the parties to settle on the eve of trial, which is super fun when you've been up all night for weeks preparing stuff for trial.

Trial and Beyond. In rare cases, you'll actually get to go to trial. This is more or less like you've seen on TV, except waaaay less dramatic. Each side will call witnesses, ask them questions, and try to get documents into evidence. Of course, the partners will be doing all the talking. But at least you might get to hand them documents?

Anyway, after both sides lay out their evidence, the jury (or judge, if it's a bench trial) will decide who prevails on each claim and then award any damages, a.k.a. money that the losing party has to pay to the other side. Following that, the losing party can appeal, which I'll talk more about in the next section.

So that's litigation in a nutshell: months or years of grunt work, with a 2-3% chance of getting to the "good" bit.

Appellate

Once the trial verdict is delivered by the judge or jury, the losing party can appeal to a higher court. The higher court, also known as an appellate court, doesn't do another trial, but instead looks to see if there were any egregious issues in how the trial judge applied the law to the facts or managed the case. If the case is especially important or tricky, the appellate judges — usually a panel of three — will hear oral argument, where lawyers from each side will lay out their arguments and answer any questions from the judges.

Appellate briefs can be fun to work on, since you get to focus on the writing without worrying about creating the record (that is, the witness testimony, the physical evidence, and so forth). But to be honest, I find appellate oral argument kind of boring. After all, it's literally just a bunch of lawyers talking and arguing.

I think appellate law is technically a branch of litigation, but believe me when I say that appellate lawyers are a special breed. They're known for being socially awkward and often snobby, even more so than the average lawyer. I'm generalizing, of course, but still. Not by that much. In their defense, they can afford to be, since they're generally brilliant. So unless you get on law review and clerk for an federal appellate judge — both of which are notoriously difficult, even if you go to a top school — don't even think about it.

My favorite appellate lawyers have been those who also practice trial law, because they're both brilliant and down-to-earth in a way that lawyers who spend all day in theoretical legal la-la land are not. One of the appellate/trial lawyers I know has talked about getting flak from appellate-only lawyers, because he's supposedly diluting his practice by not being "pure" appellate. Did I mention appellate lawyers are an elitist bunch?

Corporate

Where litigation involves analyzing cases and negotiating settlement, corporate work, a.k.a. transactional law, involves analyzing contracts and other corporate submissions (like SEC filings and prospectuses) and negotiating deals. You will spend your formative years writing up and obsessively proofing what other people have agreed to.

In litigation, junior associates may be asked to draft a settlement agreement, with the key terms given to them by a senior associate. Those are generally fairly straightforward, as the premise is always the same: Company A agrees to drop all claims against Company B for x amount of money (though Company B of course does not admit to liability).

Corporate deals can be much more difficult because there's no such template. It could be a merger, or one company selling assets to another, or a complex loan transaction. There are likely to be several different "if/then" scenarios (e.g., if Company A fails to pay in full by x date, Company B will take ownership of y assets), there may be different stages to the transaction, and/or there could be different agreements for different geographic markets. Not to mention, there are a *lot* of numbers. And I don't mean that flippantly: typos and ambiguity in contracts have cost companies **millions of dollars**,[39] and it'll be your job to make sure every single one of those numbers is correct.

---

[39] For instance, a misplaced decimal cost Lockheed Martin $70 million dollars when the customer held Lockheed to the miswritten price. Simon Watkins, "Typing Error Cost Lockheed Pounds 43M," *The Independent,* June 19, 1999, https://www.independent.co.uk/news/typing-error-cost-lockheed-pounds -43m-1100991.html.

In another case, the lack of a comma forced a company to pay $5 million in overtime to workers who were intended to be exempt. Jeff Haden, "How 1 Missing Comma Just Cost This Company $5 Million (But Did Make Its Employees $5 Million Richer)," *Inc.com,* February 12, 2018, https://www.inc.com/jeff-haden/how-1-missing-comma-just-cost-this -company-5-million-but-did-make-its-employees-5-million-richer.html.

So brush up on your grammar and proofreading skills!

Remember how I said there's no room for mistakes? Yeah.

You'll also need to make sure that all the paperwork is ready for the closing. A "closing" is just what it sounds like: it's the day that a deal officially closes. While getting paperwork ready might sound fairly straightforward, there is a *ton* of paperwork involved with closings, and you can bet that there will be revisions going back and forth until the very last minute.

You'll also be responsible for doing the initial due diligence prior to the deal, which mostly means researching the companies involved in the transaction for any potential issues. For instance, I helped with due diligence in several mergers through my work in international trade law, which involved reviewing contracts with foreign entities for any red flags, like whether the other company might have done trade with countries under U.S. economic sanctions, which is prohibited by the Office of Foreign Assets Control (OFAC), or used commission agents in transactions with foreign governments, which raises potential Foreign Corrupt Practices Act (FCPA) concerns. It's the transactional version of doc review.

As in litigation, there will often be times when you won't get any sleep, but my understanding is that those times will at least be slightly more predictable (i.e., closings). The downside is that your workflow is less assured in corporate than litigation — there's pretty much always someone suing someone else, but corporate deals depend on business being good. And at least at a big law firm, you can't just switch back and forth based on where the work is. Huzzah for involuntary specialization (not).

Regulatory

"Regulatory law," also called administrative law, refers to a smorgasbord of legal work that involves government agencies, such as international trade, environmental and energy issues, telecommunications, banking and tax, immigration, education, and employment. Because each agency operates differently, depending on its "organic statute" (that's lawyerspeak for the law that created the agency), the work varies accordingly.

And even within each subject area, there are a variety of specialties. For instance, within international trade, there is legal work ranging from ensuring compliance with customs laws and economic sanctions to defending clients undergoing white-collar criminal investigations involving the FCPA. You can also do either more litigation-type work, since many agencies have their own judges, or more corporate-type work, since corporate transactions, such as mergers, are often subject to agency scrutiny.

One interviewee notes that it can be easier to draw boundaries for your schedule in regulatory practice, since you're not necessarily dealing with the same constant, high-stress deadlines as in litigation or transactional work. However, it's important to note that this is only true for *some* types of regulatory practice. I interviewed for a regulatory position where it seemed like everyone had been working 18 hours a day for months. I didn't take the job.

Just remember that whatever type of practice you choose, you're still dealing with lawyers. And if they aren't your people, then nothing else really matters.

Chapter 10: Life in Other Legal Environments

Now that I've beaten the terror of biglaw into you, let's talk about what else is out there. I'm mostly going to talk about government, since that's what I'm familiar with, but believe me, I've looked into all the options, so I'll tell you what I know.

Clerkships

A clerkship is when you work for a judge for a year or two soon after you graduate law school (you can intern for a judge before or during law school, but that's just an internship). In clerking for a judge, you'll research and draft opinions for them and see how things are done behind the scenes. Depending on the judge, it can be a great experience. But it does depend on the judge, because you're going to spend 99% of your time in their chambers (don't worry, that just means their office suite).

You can clerk for any kind of judge — and there are a lot of different kinds — but the post-clerkship job benefits vary, at least at big law firms. Most of them will give you at least $50,000 for a federal clerkship; some will also give you a bonus if you clerk at the highest state court. (Remember what I said about everything having a ranking?) You'll also get class-year credit at firms if your clerkship is eligible, which is usually determined on the same basis as bonuses.

In other words, if you clerk for a federal judge for a year, you'd start at the firm as a second-year associate, with the commensurate salary.

So far, I've been talking about term clerkships, which are basically limited-term judicial apprenticeships. But it's also possible to be a career clerk, meaning that it's your long-term job, not just for a year or two. From what I've seen, it seems like a pretty cushy gig, but when the judge retires, you're stuck: either you have to look for another career clerkship (and there's definitely no guarantee that there will be one in the same geographic area), or you have to try to convince other legal employers that you have marketable skills despite not practicing advocacy. Yikes.

Government

Ah, the government. Refuge of the weary biglaw lawyer. Or is it? You're going to hate me for all the times I say "it depends" in this chapter, but... it depends. Whether you'd be happy in government depends entirely where you go within government and why you want to be there. I know some people who work the same hours that I did at a big law firm for less money, but they don't mind because they like that government work is more mission-oriented and free from billable hours and demanding clients. On the flip side, I know lawyers in government who do basically have 9-to-5 jobs.

I also know people who went into government and then left to go to a firm because they couldn't stand the government bureaucracy and complacency of co-workers who know they can do crappy work and still keep their jobs.

Everything you've heard about the inefficiency of government is true. For instance, when I started my agency job, I couldn't even log on to my computer until the third day I was there. Which meant that I had virtually nothing to do for two and a half days. This is a sad but true story. I also have the usual stories about things taking an absurdly long time to get done and offices passing the buck back and forth until I want to scream. It's very easy to get worn down and sucked into the bureaucratic molasses.

But let's say you're fine with the bureaucracy and want a government job. Getting a government job is itself no easy feat. Even with my credentials and experience, it took me over a year from when I started applying. And I got that job in large part because I knew the person who had the job before me.

There are two ways to get a job in the federal government: You can either get in through the Honors Program right after law school, which is insanely competitive, or you have to wait for years while you get experience elsewhere. But once you get your foot in the door, the ecstasy of being free from billable hours is no joke. You lose that constant anxious feeling of either being too busy or not busy enough. And people have time to be nice. It's not that people at law firms are necessarily mean or selfish (though some are) — they're just too busy.

Granted, there are definitely fewer material perks in government than in the private sector. No free coffee, no events with free food, and definitely no ridiculous clerkship bonuses.

On the other hand, you get more non-material benefits, like subsidized public transit, different options for flexible work schedules, and random discounts. Plus, if you want to be in court all the time, becoming a prosecutor is your best bet.[40] A friend of mine worked in the DA's office (state prosecutor) and as an AUSA (federal prosecutor), and if her experience is any indication, you get a lot of experience quickly as a state prosecutor, but the work-life balance is better in federal.

But yeah, bureaucracy.

---

[40] There is, of course, the converse: becoming a public defender. But few people are cut out for that, and if you are, you probably already know it.

Small law firms

Aside from literally having fewer people than a big law firm, other characteristics of a small law firm are completely dependent on the individual firm. Some small law firms work you just as hard as a big law firm, but for less money. Others really do support work-life balance. But it's hard to know the difference just from interviewing, so you either need to get the inside scoop somehow (see Chapter 14 on networking) or take your chances.

That said, one upside of small firms is that they give you more opportunities for responsibility earlier. For instance, I interviewed with a small firm that emphasized that they start you early on client development — that is, having you try to win new clients. I was awed and, to be honest, a little daunted by how put-together and articulate their associates were. But for folks who want to do everything as soon as possible (and without government bureaucracy), you might have a better shot at a small firm.

Non-traditional law firms

One of my interviewees, Max, used to be a solo practitioner, which he enjoyed because it allowed him to be his own boss. Now he's working at a non-traditional law firm that operates on a flat-fee basis.

According to Max, his new job "has a lot of what I liked about working for myself": he works from home, he has flexible hours, and he's compensated for work done rather than hours billed. Moreover, because he's rewarded for efficiency through the alternative fee structure, he's able to set up processes to streamline the more repetitive aspects of his work, rather than having to sacrifice efficiency in order to meet billable hour requirements. As a bonus, he no longer faces the pressure of figuring out his own marketing and overhead.

But before you get too excited about the prospect of non-traditional law firms, they're still few and far between. Plus, if you want to do anything besides contracts, doc review, and/or patent prosecution (not to be confused with patent litigation), they're pretty much nonexistent. And while some of them, like Max's, might be good, others are really, really not.[41]

In-house

Being in-house counsel means that you're an attorney who works at and represents a specific organization. Most, if not all, companies have in-house counsel, but how many

---

[41] *See, e.g.,* Carolyn Elefant, "When #Altlaw Is Bad, It Is Truly Horrid," *Above the Law,* February 22, 2018, https://abovethelaw.com/2018/02/when-altlaw-is-bad-it-is-truly-horrid/.

attorneys they have will vary. A big corporation like Facebook likely has a huge legal department, with different specialty groups. On the other hand, a small nonprofit might only have one attorney who does everything.

Similarly, the actual work you'd do depends on the company and the size of the legal department. But it does require knowing as much about the business as you do about the law, if not more, so you'd better make sure you're interested in the business, especially since it's now your only client. On top of that, you'll be expected to opine on areas of law you know nothing about. And while you're free from the billable hour, you're the one responsible for managing any catastrophes that arise. (Imagine being in-house counsel at General Motors when the ignition switch scandal came to light, or at BP when the Deepwater Horizon oil spill happened.)

Corporations generally prefer to hire attorneys with transactional background, since litigation stuff is mostly handled by outside counsel (that is, third-party law firms). Granted, that's not always the case, especially with massive companies like Google that get sued a lot, but for most companies, it will be.

That said, according to one blog post from Above the Law, "Very small companies [that only have room for one or two attorneys] will often hire litigators because business people don't have a clue about how to draft motions or deal with court deadlines."[42] The post also recommends "check[ing] out companies in certain industries, such as insurance, that handle a lot of complaints/litigation as these will tend to need more litigators."

If you want to do more work on the business side — which, fair warning, involves lots of spreadsheets, numbers, and financial data[43] — in-house is a good place to be. They usually want folks who have practiced law elsewhere first — many in-house attorneys transitioned from a law firm to a client business that they had established a relationship with — but some corporations, like HP and Pfizer, are starting to develop programs for new law school graduates.

Nonprofits

Many people assume that all nonprofits are fuzzy bunnies, but nonprofits are way more of a mixed bag than you might think. I've worked with various legal nonprofits in my pro bono work and was surprised by how uncooperative and small-minded many of those folks were.

---

[42] Susan Moon, "9 Things That May Surprise You About Going In-House," *Above the Law*, June 10, 2014, http://abovethelaw.com/2014/06/9 -things-that-may-surprise-you-about-going-in-house/.

[43] Susan Moon, "Moonlighting: Things Not to Say In-House – 'I'm Bad at Math'," *Above the Law*, January 6, 2012, http://abovethelaw.com/2012/01 /moonlighting-things-not-to-say-in-house-im-bad-at-math/.

Now, to be fair, there were also delightful nonprofit people I worked with, and I know lawyers who have gone to nonprofits and absolutely love it. You just need to be wary of any preconceptions you might have, because they're not all created equal. And if you find an awesome one, it will probably be insanely difficult to get a job, because either everyone wants to work there or the organization has no money to hire people. I know, it sucks.

Plus, even if you land a job at a nonprofit where you love the people and the mission, the work itself can still be draining. Karen, who left law after doing legal aid work for three years, says, "I felt burned out and began to feel like legal practice ... was an inefficient avenue for social change." As she put it, "I was working more than full time, barely making any money, and every time I helped one client, another would come up with the exact same problem. It felt like I was spinning my wheels."

There are a few different points in there. First, she was working long hours while making hardly any money. Going to the public sector is not a guarantee of work-life balance, just as going to a prestigious law school (Karen also went to Harvard Law) is not a guarantee of a big paycheck.

Second, she become frustrated that she wasn't making an impact beyond her individual clients. Law is a colossally slow-moving beast. Plus, as you might remember, only some courts can tell other courts what to do. (And the Supreme Court is the only one that can tell all the courts what to do.) Moreover, every case can be distinguished on its facts, so a favorable holding in one case is no guarantee of a similar holding in a seemingly identical case.

Sure, every once in a while you come across a case with huge and clear social impact, like *Brown v. Board of Education*, but cases like those are the exception, not the rule. To put it in perspective, the Supreme Court receives about 7,000-8,000 petitions for a writ of certiorari each Term, but only grants oral argument in about 80 cases.[44] So you have about a 1% chance of even getting to the Supreme Court, let alone doing so with a life-changing case.[45]

If you still think you want to pursue the nonprofit path (as many aspiring lawyers do, at least at first), feel free to poke around on the internet and see what sounds interesting to you. But remember, something can sound great on paper

---

[44] "FAQs – General Information," Supreme Court of the United States (website), accessed July 4, 2018, https://www.supremecourt.gov/about/faq_general.aspx.

[45] Many of the cases the Supreme Court hears are actually not that interesting, at least in my opinion. But hey, maybe you're interested in whether the Foreign Sovereign Immunities Act bars a U.S. citizen from bringing suit against an Austrian railroad in federal district court, or whether a disgorgement payment is subject to a five-year statute of limitations. *See OBB Personenverkehr AG v. Sachs*, 577 U.S. ___ (2015); *Kokesh v. SEC*, 581 U.S. ___ (2016).

and not be in real life. So later in the book, I'll talk about how to reach out to someone at an organization you're interested in to get a better feel for what it's like.

Part Four:

How to Figure Out If Law Is Right for You

Chapter 11: Figure It Out
Before Law School

Almost all of the people I interviewed who are still happily lawyering figured out what they wanted to do *before* they went to law school. They did their research, they worked in the real world, and they figured out — through actual experience — exactly what they wanted to do. As biglaw associate Eliza puts it, "You need to have a clear sense of why you want to be a lawyer or it gets really hard to continue, because law is not a forgiving profession."

Allison, a non-equity partner[46] at a big law firm, agrees, noting that a lot of people "jump into law school without knowing what they want to do," when they should figure out what they want to do first. Otherwise, she points out, you lose those critical early years when you're establishing your practice area. After all, law is a professional school. It's not just the next thing after high school and college; you're training to be ready for your job. How can you do that effectively if you don't know what your job is going to be?

---

[46] Traditionally, if you made partner, usually around your tenth year, you were automatically granted a piece of the law firm's profits (equity). But some law firms now make associates non-equity partners around their sixth year, presumably to make clients feel important by having several partners on their case and get them to pay more.

So in this section, I'm going to talk about how to figure out if law is right for you. You'll have to put in effort, but it's better to do it now instead of when you're miserable and carrying a ridiculous amount of debt, right?

Chapter 12: Look Inward First

This chapter was inspired by one of my interviewees, career coach and blogger Casey Berman. Initially, I had planned to just dive into the advice about researching jobs and networking (I know, everyone's favorite word). But after talking with Casey about the advice he gives to lawyers thinking about leaving law, I realized that before you can know whether law school is right for you, you have to know yourself.

Sure, you probably know the basics, like what subjects and activities you like or dislike. But do you know what you need in a work environment? Do you know what core skills you have that you'll want to use at work? You might know a couple, like writing or public speaking, but most of us have more than one or two skills that we'll need to use at work regularly in order to feel fulfilled.

On top of that, college is a time of formative change. It's the first time you're not under your parents' roof (at least for most people), and, academically speaking, you get to explore areas of learning beyond a set curriculum for the first time. So even if you thought law school was the right path for you in high school, that doesn't mean it will continue to be the right path as you spread your proverbial wings.

So what do you do now? (Hint: Keep reading.)

Your Unique Genius

Once again, I'm going to steal from Casey, who recommends focusing on your Unique Genius.[47] Your Unique Genius, as you can probably guess from the name, is what you are uniquely good at. Identifying your Unique Genius is harder than knowing generally what you're good at, because you might be very good at a lot of things. But your Unique Genius is at the intersection of what you love doing and what other people consider you to be the best at.

The Hedgehog Concept. To clarify what your Unique Genius is — and, more importantly, what it isn't — let's talk about the "Hedgehog Concept" from *Good to Great* by Jim Collins.[48] Collins defines it as "a simple, crystalline concept that flows from deep understanding about the intersection" of three key elements:

---

[47] Casey Berman, "The Third Step in Leaving Law Behind – Do What You Are Good At," *Leave Law Behind,* March 29, 2013, http://leavelawbehind.com/2013/03/29/the-third-step-in-leaving-law -behind-do-what-you-are-good-at/; Casey Berman, "A Valuable Lesson from Last Week's Leave Law Behind Event," *Leave Law Behind,* October 8, 2012, http://leavelawbehind.com/2012/10/08/a-valuable -lesson-from-last-weeks-leave-law-behind-event/.

[48] Jim Collins, *Good to Great: Why Some Companies Make the Leap... and Others Don't* (New York: HarperCollins, 2001). If you're curious, the name comes from the essay "The Hedgehog and the Fox" by Isaiah Berlin. But it's otherwise irrelevant.

1. What you can be the best in the world at;

2. What drives your economic engine; and

3. What you are deeply passionate about.[49]

In the book, the Hedgehog Concept is what propelled companies from good to great, but it can also be extended to people.[50] Your Unique Genius is #1, what you can be the best in the world at. However, as Collins makes clear, "what you can be the best in the world at" is not the same as what you *want* to be the best at.[51] Likewise, it's "not a goal to the best, a strategy to be the best, an intention to be the best, a plan to be the best."[52] Rather, it's an *understanding* of what you can be the best at.[53]

What you can be the best at is also not the same as what you're competent — even extremely competent — at.[54] It is only what you have the potential to become the *best* at. That's why it's your "Unique Genius." By definition, your Unique Genius is what you are uniquely and instinctively amazing at. When I was younger, I thought I could be the

---

[49] Collins, *Good to Great,* 90-119 (italics omitted).
[50] Collins, 96.
[51] Collins, 118.
[52] Collins, 98.
[53] Collins, 98.
[54] Collins, 100.

best at lawyering. But as I got closer to the top, I realized that I could never be the best because my talents (writing, analytical thinking, public speaking) weren't enough to compensate for my shortcomings (I'm not great at thinking on my feet or issue-spotting). So after leaving law, I had to figure out where my strengths would be a better fit across the board.

Regarding #2, what drives your economic engine, I believe that you will discover opportunities to make money as a natural effect of focusing on what you're uniquely good at. Both Casey Berman and financial guru Ramit Sethi contend that once you know your value, the money will follow. Casey also points out that there are a ton of jobs where you can make excellent money — while law happens to be one of the more prominent ones, it's definitely not the only one.

More importantly, taking a job just for the money will make you unhappy.[55] For instance, one meta-analysis, involving 120 years of research from 92 quantitative studies, shows that "the association between salary and job satisfaction is very weak," with less than a 2% overlap

---

[55] To get a better understanding of why that is, I recommend reading Daniel Pink's excellent book, *Drive: The Surprising Truth About What Motivates Us*, which discusses the difference between intrinsic and extrinsic motivation. (Spoiler alert: You'll be happier if you have more of the first kind, and money usually falls into the second category.)

between pay and job satisfaction, *and* only a 4.8% overlap between pay and pay satisfaction.[56] In other words, even getting paid what you want doesn't necessarily mean you'll be happy with the money!

As for #3 of the Hedgehog Concept, what you are deeply passionate about, we'll talk about that more in next chapter.

What Is Your Unique Genius? To figure out what your Unique Genius is, ask:

1. What are you already doing (or would you do) for free to help people?

2. For what type of advice do people come to you?

3. What do people compliment you on?

You need to rope other people into this to get the most out of it. You might feel weird about asking people for compliments, but since your friends like you, they're probably happy to help. Even my insanely busy lawyer friends responded in a matter of minutes.

---

[56] Tomas Chamorro-Premuzic, "Does Money Really Affect Motivation? A Review of the Research," *Harvard Business Review*, April 10, 2013. https://hbr.org/2013/04/does-money-really-affect-motiv. *See also* Phyllis Korkki, "Job Satisfaction vs. a Big Paycheck," *New York Times*, September 11, 2010, http://www.nytimes.com2010/09/12/jobs/12search.html.

If you don't feel comfortable doing it in person, just send them a quick text — don't send a group text though, that will get out of hand, and it'll also deprive you of independent responses — saying something like, "I'll explain later, but can you please tell me 3 things you think I'm good at?"

Once you have your list, organize those traits and skills into buckets.[57] For each bucket, you'll probably have an umbrella category like "People skills," with more specific sub-traits like "Good listener" and "Makes new people feel welcome." Categorize your skills however it makes sense to you, aiming for around 3-5 buckets.

Casey recommends turning those 3-5 buckets of traits and/or skills into a narrative of your Unique Genius.[58] While he suggests doing that so you can (a) find jobs that align with your Unique Genius and (b) present your Unique Genius succinctly and persuasively during job interviews, having a coherent self-narrative isn't just for your job hunt: **it can actually improve your well-being.**

Rebecca Schlegel and her colleagues in personality and social psychology have shown that we perceive our lives as

---

[57] Casey Berman, "My 21 Step Guide on How to Leave the Law and Begin Anew," *Leave Law Behind*, April 23, 2015, http://leavelawbehind .com/2015/04/23/my-21-step-guide-on-how-to-leave-the-law-and-begin -anew/.

[58] Berman, "My 21 Step Guide."

having more meaning when we have a strong sense of self.[59] That's true even when we're thinking about our flaws.[60]

Even better, when we feel connected to our true selves, we're "less likely to conform to the preferences of others [...]."[61] What do I mean by our "true selves"? To paraphrase Dr. Schlegel, your true self is who you really are, even if you don't always act accordingly.[62] A study on conformity and the self by Jamie Arndt and team concluded that "self-esteem derived from intrinsic and stable self-characteristics leads to [...] greater self-determination than does self-esteem that is contingent on a sense of [extrinsic] achievement or accomplishment."[63]

This distinction between intrinsic and extrinsic self-esteem, or self-worth, is critical. Intrinsic self-worth is based

---

[59] Rebecca J. Schlegel et al., "Thine Own Self: True Self-Concept Accessibility and Meaning in Life." *Journal of Personality and Social Psychology* 96, no. 2 (2009); Rebecca J. Schlegel et al., "Feeling Like You Know Who You Are: Perceived True Self-Knowledge and Meaning in Life," *Personality and Social Psychology Bulletin* 37, no. 6 (March 2011).

[60] Schlegel et al., "Thine Own Self," 485 ("[E]ven negative words that describe the true self-concept appear to serve as a source of meaning.").

[61] Arndt et al., "The Intrinsic Self and Defensiveness: Evidence That Activating the Intrinsic Self Reduces Self-Handicapping and Conformity," *Personality and Social Psychology Bulletin* 28, no. 5 (May 2002): 679.

[62] *See* Schlegel et al., "Thine Own Self," 482.

[63] Arndt et al., 380.

on who you really are (or at least you believe you really are), i.e., your true self. Extrinsic self-worth is based on what you've achieved. And according to Dr. Arndt's conformity study, when your feelings of self-worth are based on your true self, rather than your achievements, you're less likely to conform to what others think.

Conversely (and content warning for suicide in this paragraph), social psychologist Roy Baumeister has argued that suicide is generally caused by "high standards and expectations combined with current, specific failures, setbacks, or stresses" — i.e., failures to achieve — that you blame on yourself.[64] Baumeister also notes that "suicidal college students have typically had better grades and often higher parental expectations than other college students."[65]

I'm so sorry for suddenly going morbid, but this point bears making. You are more than your achievements. I'm sure they're awesome, and you should take pride in them. But if you've defined yourself as an achiever, what happens when you fail? Failing is good, because it means you're trying. But if you're not used to it, it can also be jarring as

---

[64] Roy F. Baumeister, "Suicide as Escape From Self," *Psychological Review* 97, no. 1 (January 1990): 91.

[65] Baumeister, 94.

hell. That's why you need a self-narrative based on who you are, not just what you've achieved.

"But how do I even create a self-narrative?" you ask in anguish. Don't worry, I got you. See next chapter.

Chapter 13: Personal Mission Statement

In this chapter, I'm going to walk you through how to write a personal mission statement, a.k.a. your self-narrative.

There's no right or wrong way to do a personal mission statement. It doesn't even have to be an essay-like thing, although that's what I'm going to talk about here. It can be a picture, a poem, a story — whatever helps to clarify the best way forward for you. So feel free to modify what I've suggested, or even do something completely different. What I've outlined below is an amalgamation of what I've found to be most useful from various sources on this topic.[66]

There are two levels to my approach: the foundational level, based on your true self, and the higher level, which is your mission in life (don't worry if you don't know what your mission is yet; that's what the foundation is for!). The purpose of the foundation approach is to figure out, as fully as possible, who your true self is. Remember, the stronger your sense of self, the more benefit you get out of it.

Then, with the higher level, you can build on that to figure out where you want to go from here. Remember, life is a

_____

[66] One worth mentioning is the Franklin Covey personal mission statement builder, available for free at https://msb.franklincovey.com/. You fill in responses to prompts, and it compiles them into a personal mission statement. It's pretty nifty.

journey, not a destination, so you want to make sure that you're happy with the direction you're heading in.

Foundational level

The foundational level has three parts: (1) Unique Genius; (2) Needs; and (3) Passions.

Unique Genius (Again). We already talked in the last chapter about how to figure out what your Unique Genius is, so I'm not going to spend too much time on it here. The most important thing to remember is that your Unique Genius is not what you *want* to be best at, but what you *can* be best at. The second most important thing to remember is that it's not just what you can be really good at, but what you can be *best* at.

Needs. According to Gallup, people who "have the opportunity to focus on their strengths every day are six times as likely to be engaged in their jobs and more than three times as likely to report having excellent quality of life in general."[67]

However, every strength has needs. We all have days where, even if we're doing something that we're innately

---

[67] Tom Rath, *StrengthFinders 2.0* (New York: Gallup, 2007), III (emphasis in original).

good at, we're just not bringing our A-game. That's because we need certain conditions in order to perform at our best. For instance, as I mentioned earlier, getting enough sleep is crucial for me. Otherwise, I'm just a cranky zombie. And while I prefer to work independently, if I go too long without human interaction, I get stir-crazy.

In short, your needs are whatever is required to bring your best self to the table. Once you figure out what your needs are, you'll have a better sense of what to look for in your next workplace. Are your hours flexible? Do you get your own space? Are there structured opportunities for you to get to know your colleagues and find mentors?

If you're not sure what your needs are, here's a prompt adapted from StrengthsFinder. Think of some activities or experiences you had that you found either fulfilling or frustrating. For each activity or experience, why was it fulfilling or frustrating? In particular, what conditions were present in the fulfilling experiences that were absent in the frustrating ones, and vice versa?

Obviously there will be some conditions you'll never be able to control for, like stupid, annoying, and/or incompetent people. But hopefully you'll see a pattern of things you *can* have a say in. For instance, I'm much better under pressure if I know in advance that it's coming down the pipeline or if such emergencies are infrequent. And that's definitely something I can look for in my job search. While you might not be able to have every need met, you can at least know, and look for, optimal workplace conditions.

Passions. The last building block of the foundational level is what you're passionate about. As Collins explains in *Good to Great*, you can't force yourself to feel passionate about something; you can only figure out what you're passionate about.[68]

Ask yourself: What can you talk about for hours without getting bored? If you didn't have to worry about money, what would you do all day? (Or rather, what would you do all day after you got sick of binge-watching television and scrolling through social media?)

Another way to figure out what you're passionate about is to notice when you're in a state of "flow." Coined by psychologist Mihaly Csikszentmihalyi, flow refers to those times when you're "in the zone," actively engaged in whatever you're doing, until you look up and it's suddenly 4 hours later. (To be clear, the time should pass because you're mentally absorbed, not because you're working so frantically that you haven't had time to go to the bathroom.)

---

[68] Collins, *Good to Great*, 109.

As Dr. Lyubomirsky describes in *The How of Happiness*, "Flow is a way of describing an experience that falls in just the right space between boredom [from being too easy] and anxiety [from being too difficult]."[69] Put another way, flow involves effort without strain — you're challenging yourself, but it feels good, like a satisfying workout. Hard, but not too hard.

To be clear, being passionate about something doesn't mean that it makes you happy all the time, or that you find it easy. But it should always bring you joy to have done it. Joy is what happens when you realize that you feel fulfilled. It's not merely the satisfaction of a job well done, but the warm-glow feeling that comes from engaging your true self. In other words, it feels like you're being who you're meant to be.

This requires your work to be *meaningful*. Now, meaningful does not necessarily mean working at a nonprofit to save the whales or whatever. So if you're like, "Er... I'm not sure I'm that good of a person," don't worry. When I say "meaningful," I mean meaningful *to you* — that is, something you care about, not something you think you *should* care about. (Sorry, whales.)

---

[69] Lyubomirsky, *How of Happiness*, 181-182.

Something is meaningful if it holds emotional resonance for you. You don't just like it on a superficial level; you feel a deep connection to it. For me, writing is a part of my identity, even though I often find it ridiculously difficult. While this is the first book I've published, I've been writing since I learned the alphabet, and I have an unintelligible story I wrote in kindergarten about a cat and a rat to prove it. Writing has been a constant theme throughout my life, and it feels right when I'm doing it.

Speaking of which, if you get stuck at any point, try freewriting. Set a timer for 10 minutes or so, set all your devices to "Do Not Disturb," and write (or type) the whole time. Don't worry about spelling and grammar, don't revise or reread what you wrote — that's your inner editor trying to sneak in — and just write. Your hands shouldn't stop moving, even if you just type the last word over and over or write about how stuck you are.

Once you've done some deep thinking about your Unique Genius, needs, and passions, you should have a much clearer sense of who you are and what motivates you. Then, in the next section, we'll talk about using that to figure out where to go from here.

Higher level

Now that you've laid the foundation by developing a clearer picture of your true self, it's time to think about the best way forward. This section will help you figure out how and where you want to channel your energy. Since your energy is finite, it's crucial to make sure that you're spending it wisely. To that end, let's talk about the higher level, which has two interdependent parts: Purpose and Goals.

Purpose. Your purpose is your anchor. It gives your life meaning, so you're not just going through the motions each day.

I would suggest that right now, your purpose is to find work that brings you joy. That means: (1) using your Unique Genius (2) in an environment that enables you to perform at your best (3) in an area that you're passionate about. Yup, that's the foundational level we just talked about.

One way to clarify your purpose is by doing the famous funeral eulogy exercise from Stephen Covey's *7 Habits of Highly Effective People*.[70] Imagine people from different aspects of your life (family, friends, work, and community)

---

[70] Stephen R. Covey, *The 7 Habits of Highly Effective People: Powerful Lessons in Personal Change*, 25th anniversary ed. (New York: Simon & Schuster, 2004), 103-104.

speaking at your funeral about the legacy you've left behind. How do you want to be remembered? What do you want to be remembered for? And what do you need to do to make that a reality?

Goals. Now that you have an idea of your purpose, it's time to figure how to get there from here. That's where your goals come in.

Think of your purpose as where you want to go. Now you need to plan how to get there. Your goals are the to-dos in your plan. If you wanted to go to Europe, you'd have to get a bunch of things in order before you went, right? You'd need to sort out your passport, figure out your itinerary, buy tickets, pack, etc. And along the way, things will probably change. You might try to fit in another stop, or maybe you'll look at the weather forecast and realize it's going to be colder than you thought, so you have to re-think your packing.

It's the same with life goals. Making a plan is important to ensure that you have a direction (or, dare I say, purpose) and aren't just aimlessly wandering. But things can change, either in terms of your circumstances or what you want, and that's okay. Just make a plan for now, with the understanding that you can always revise it later.

There are tangible benefits to writing down your goals. First, it's "associated with feeling less upset, more happy, and getting sick less often."[71] Second, writing down our goals strengthens our commitment to them. That's because we feel more responsible for pledges that are made actively rather than passively, and even the simple act of writing your goals down means that you're doing something related to your goals ("doing" being the operative word). One study found that participants who actively wrote down their commitment to volunteer in a future project, versus passively not opting out, were far more likely to follow through.[72]

As Dr. Lyubomirsky explains:

> Because writing is highly structured, systematic, and rule-bound, it prompts you to organize, integrate, and analyze your thoughts in a way that would be difficult, if not impossible, to do if you were just [thinking about it]. Writing about your goals helps you put your thoughts together in a coherent manner, allowing you to find meaning in your life experiences. ... This new understanding may provide you with a

---

[71] Laura A. King, "The Health Benefits of Writing About Life Goals," *Personality and Social Psychology Bulletin* 27, no. 7 (July 2001): 804-05.

[72] Noah J. Goldstein, Steve J. Martin, and Robert B. Cialdini, *Yes! 50 Scientifically Proven Ways to Be Persuasive* (New York: Free Press, 2008), 76-77.

feeling of control ... and help you recognize and reduce conflict among your goals and the obstacles that might stand in your way...[73]

Studies have also shown that making a plan helps manage stress and reduce intrusive thoughts.[74] But there are two caveats. First, while planning helps keep you from getting mentally overwhelmed, it does not alleviate negative *emotions*,[75] which is why I recommend that you journal your anxieties separately. (More on that in Chapter 16, when we talk about what to do if you've decided not to go to law school.)

Second, to get the cognitive benefits of planning, the plan has to be specific — you have to clearly define the actions you're going to take, and when and where you'll take

---

[73] Lyubomirsky, *How of Happiness*, 105.

[74] Marina Watson Peláez, "Plan Your Way to Less Stress, More Happiness," *TIME.com*, May 31, 2011, http://healthland.time.com/2011/05/31/study-25 -of-happiness-depends-on-stress-management/ ("The stress management technique that worked best, according to the survey: planning."); E.J. Masicampo, and Roy F. Baumeister, "Consider It Done! Plan Making Can Eliminate the Cognitive Effects of Unfulfilled Goals," *Journal of Personality and Social Psychology* 101, no. 4 (October 2011).

[75] Masicampo and Baumeister, 679.

them.[76] I like the S.M.A.R.T. goals mnemonic, which advises you to set goals that are:

1. <u>S</u>pecific — Who, what, where, when, etc. It's not enough to merely "reflect[] on the various ways" of fulfilling your goals or to generally intend "to pursue a goal";[77] you have to commit to a particular course of action. The more specific, the better.

2. <u>M</u>easurable — What kind of metric are you going to use to determine if you've met your goal? Make it quantifiable if possible. Otherwise, tie it to something tangible in the real world that you can point to as evidence of success. Either way, you should be able to clearly tell if you've achieved your goal or not.

3. <u>A</u>chievable — Is your goal realistic? Trying to become an Olympic skier when you just learned how to navigate the bunny slopes last week is probably not a recipe for success.

4. <u>R</u>elevant — Does this goal in fact further your purpose? This might seem like a silly question, especially after all the work you've just done, but it's surprisingly easy to think that something "sounds

---

[76] Masicampo and Baumeister, 680 ("[R]eflecting on various potential plans of action [i]s not sufficient to reduce activation from unfulfilled goals. Rather, one must have committed to a specific plan of action [...] .").

[77] Masicampo and Baumeister, 679 & 668.

good" without making sure that it connects to what you're ultimately trying to accomplish. In other words, why *this* goal?

5. <u>T</u>ime-bound — Set a deadline (or several). By when are you going to accomplish what?

For example, maybe you're still considering law school, and you've decided that your purpose is to find work that brings you joy. But in trying to fulfill that purpose, you've realized you need to think more critically about what area of law you'd want to go into, and you're feeling overwhelmed by all the options.

Your initial goal might look like this: "I'll figure out what practice area(s) I'm interested in." But that's too vague. How are you going to figure out what areas you're interested in? What kind of research are you going to do?

If you're not sure where to start, use Google. I googled "legal practice areas" just to see what turned up, and I found great resources on the first page. And when you find a practice area that sounds interesting, google that next. Then, if you want to know more, you can use the tips in the next chapter to reach out to someone who works in that area of law.

So, using the S.M.A.R.T. criteria, here's what your refined goal might look like: "By September 30, I will identify 3 practice areas I'm interested in, reach out to at least 2 people in each field through LinkedIn, and arrange at least 1 in-person informational interview." You've set a deadline, you've made it quantifiable, and you'll know without a doubt on September 30 if you've reached your goal.

Or maybe you've realized that you're not quite ready to commit to law school yet. Your initial goal might look something like this: "I will research alternative career possibilities that allow me to use my talents in public speaking and persuasive writing." But again, this isn't specific enough. What will researching entail? How will you decide when you're done? Plus, you'll definitely need to narrow the parameters of your search, since there are about a bazillion jobs that involve public speaking and persuasive writing.

So let's try it again with the S.M.A.R.T. criteria. Set a deadline, get specific and quantifiable, and make sure it's rooted in your purpose. Now your goal might look more like this: "By June 30, I will identify 3 potential alternative careers based on my Unique Genius and passions, reach out to 5 people on LinkedIn in those areas, and set up at least 2 informational interviews."

Way better, right? You know the specific steps you're going to take, you know when you're going to take them by, and when June 30 rolls around, you'll know whether you've accomplished your goal. In the next chapter, we'll talk more about how to research jobs, so if you're feeling overwhelmed, don't worry.

To sum up: Your purpose is where you want to go, so figure out what your goals need to be to get there, *write them down*, and make a S.M.A.R.T. plan for how to achieve them.

Putting it all together

At this point, if you haven't already, you should set aside time to actually write your personal mission statement. It's okay if it's hard, or if you're not sure if you "did it right." It's an iterative process, especially when it comes to your purpose and goals, which will evolve over time as you accomplish things, learn more about what you do and don't like, and correct your course accordingly.

It's a good idea to have both a long and short version of your mission statement. The long version is for when you're thinking deeply about What's Next. The short version is for when you just need a quick reminder to find your focus again.

Here's one of my favorite inspirational quotes to help you get motivated:

> **"Never give up on a dream just because
> of the time it will take to accomplish it.
> The time will pass anyway."**

Chapter 14: Now Do Your Research

Now that you have your purpose and goals, it's time to get down to the nitty-gritty of actually researching jobs. I'll assume that you're still thinking about law school, though the general strategies will also be helpful if you've been swayed by my words of wisdom and are now considering other options.

To find out what being a lawyer is actually like, there are a few ways to go about it: (1) do informational interviews; (2) work for a legal organization; and (3) job-shadow.

LinkedIn

Before we discuss how to get exposure to the legal profession, let's talk about the best place to start your career exploration: LinkedIn. If you're not familiar with LinkedIn, it's basically a social media website for professionals. Luckily, you can create an account even if you're still in school, and your university's career counselors can probably help.

Similar to Facebook, everyone on LinkedIn has a profile. While a lot of profiles just have basic information about the person's educational background and work experience, others are much more detailed and can be helpful in your career search. (Unlike Facebook though, personal or silly photos are *not* okay to use on your profile. If you don't have a professional-looking photo — which is totally fine and normal if you're still in school — just leave the photo box empty.)

You can search by keywords, such as duties and responsibilities, not just job title and company. Just go to Advanced Search, then type the job tasks or other criteria you're looking for. You can even use this opportunity to try a free 30-day trial of LinkedIn Premium, which will give you access to profiles that you might not otherwise be able to see. (Hat tip to career guru Ashley Stahl for this technique.) An added bonus of the 30-day trial is that it forces you to take action quickly. Like most unpleasant-but-inevitable things, we know in theory that it's just better to bite the bullet and get it over with, but sometimes we need a little push to get started.

"But wait," you say. "I don't even know what job tasks to put in there."

I have two words for you: Unique Genius. And so it comes full circle.

Use those 3-5 buckets that you came up with in the previous chapter as keywords. While those alone will get you too many hits to be directly useful, as you go through the profiles, you'll be able to see what kind of words and other criteria you can add to narrow it down.

If you're looking at legal jobs, add the word "law" or "legal." If you're interested in nonprofits, add the word "nonprofit." If you're interested in civil rights, add that. And so on and so forth.

On the other hand, if you're interested in exploring careers outside of law, you might not be able to narrow it down as quickly. But that's okay; the world is your oyster!

In either case, make sure to note the name and URL of the profiles that you find interesting. You may even want to print them out (in case the profile is only available through LinkedIn Premium) and start a file or binder. If you really want to geek out, you can arrange the binder by tabs according to the different career options you're considering.

Another way to narrow it down is to search only within the alumni at your university. I don't recommend that for general career exploration, since it's more limited, but it does increase the odds that the person you reach out to will respond. To find alumni, go to your university's LinkedIn page. The menu on the left should include an "Alumni" option. From there, in addition to the keyword search bar, you can find alumni by geographic location, major, and where they work now.

Once you find a person, job, or company that sounds interesting, that's when the three networking strategies I mentioned at the beginning of this chapter come into play.

Informational interviews

I know, "informational interview" is almost as bad as "networking" when it comes to career-advice words that make you groan and wish you were dead. Or at least independently wealthy.

I feel you, I do. Like most millennials and under, I hate talking to strangers in real life, and like many lawyers, I'm extremely introverted. But the thing is, there's no internet substitute for this. In most cases, a legal organization's website has been designed by marketing people for marketing purposes and is basically useless for getting real information. I know this because I've had *many* interviews where I've brought up something that was on the firm's website, and the interviewer replied, "Huh, really? Eh, that's just marketing."

Moreover, the internet can't really tell you what the day-to-day life is like at a specific organization. Even if you found a blog post that purports to do so, chances are that either the organization approved it or the person has a grudge. Either way, not super helpful. You want the average, unfiltered perspective, and there's no better way to do that than talking to someone in real life, where every word isn't scrutinized and polished.

At the very least, the person you interview presents an opportunity to learn more about your potential career path. That alone is a reason to go outside your comfort zone before spending thousands of dollars on law school.

On top of that, you're growing your network. Have you heard the expression "It's not what you know, it's who you know"? It's cliché, but true (as many clichés are). I got my government job in part because I went to law school with the guy who had the job before me.

The legal market is oversaturated with lawyers, many of whom have impressive resumes. The way to get the extra edge is to actually know someone where you want to work, so that when your application comes up, your contact can say, "Oh yeah, I know her! She's pretty cool, we should definitely get her in here."

It's even better if your contact is someone you *didn't* know before, because reaching out to them demonstrates both interest and initiative. Use your list of LinkedIn people as a starting point for reaching out. Another option is to check with your college's career or alumni office. I guarantee you that your college has alumni who have become lawyers, and your college can likely help you get in touch with them.

You can also ask friends and family — they might surprise you. For instance, your parents probably have a lawyer they use to keep their wills up-to-date. Even if you're not interested in wills and trusts, that lawyer knows other lawyers. If your parents work for a big company or the government, they might know one or two of the in-house lawyers.

"But how do I reach out to a complete stranger?" you ask.

The most important thing to remember is that you're asking them to do you a favor, so don't assume or act like you're entitled to their time. In most cases, they're probably happy to help, but only if it's not too inconvenient for them. Just keep your message short and to the point. These are busy people!

Introduce yourself, tell them how you found them and why you think they're awesome, and then ask if they have time for a phone call (or a coffee date if they're local), so you can benefit from the wisdom of their experience. And always err on the side of formality — they'll let you know if it's okay to call them by their first name.

Once someone says yes, you can find a ton of resources on how to do an informational interview through a basic internet search. Here are a few general tips to get you started:

Prepare. As I said, the point of an informational interview is to: (1) ensure that you get information and insights to help you decide what you want to do, and (2) leave your interviewee with a good impression in case you apply for a job there later. So do not (as I did once) request an informational meeting and then have nothing prepared because you're confident that you can make it up as you go. It's a waste of everyone's time, including yours, and you've just underwhelmed a potential contact and resource. If it's in person, be sure to dress professionally, and *definitely* don't no-show — even if there's an emergency, take two seconds to let them know, and then make sure to follow up afterwards.

Don't ask for a job. People tend to get annoyed when you ask them for a job within 10 minutes of meeting them, especially since they're doing you a favor meeting you in the first place. If they like you, they'll probably see what they can do anyway, which is all the more reason to make sure you put your best foot forward. And if a job opening is posted, by all means apply, and reach out to your interviewee to let him or her know.

Bring your resume. If you do hit it off, it helps to be prepared in case your interviewee wants to give your resume to HR. But don't go overboard with references, transcripts, etc., because that will foster the impression that you just want a job and don't really care about what your interviewee has to say.

Ideas for questions. In coming up with questions, think about what you're interested in. Again, you can get ideas from Google, but here are a few suggestions:

- What's the most interesting case they've worked on? What's the least interesting one?

- What do they spend most of their time doing? How has it changed over time?

- Do not ask them what a "typical day" is like, as 9 out of 10 lawyers will say, "There is no typical day." Because lawyers are obnoxious.

Follow up with a thank-you email. This person did you a favor. Say thank you. Just make sure to check your spelling and grammar — including whether you've spelled the person's name correctly — before you hit "Send."

Work in law

As discussed further in the next chapter, I strongly recommend that you work *anywhere* for at least 1-2 years between college and law school, especially since most law schools allow you to defer. But if you want a real glimpse into the legal profession, work for a law office. Do that for a year or two, and you'll see the good, the bad, and the ugly. I know a number of paralegals who thought they wanted to go to law school, then decided that there was no way in hell after working at a law firm.

Some law firms offer summer positions for college students, as kind of pre-paralegals. But a summer-only gig isn't enough. Sure, it looks good on your resume, and you might learn a thing or two while making decent money. But in most cases, unless you have the amazingly good fortune of helping on a big litigation or deal, it won't tell you what working at a firm is like in the long run.

For one thing, there's a horde of summer associates roaming the halls, and since the firm desperately wants to impress and recruit these law students, everyone is on their best behavior. Plus, partners go on vacation during the summer, so everyone else gets to be more relaxed. But summer is only three months out of the year, and you need to know what the other nine months are like.

Job-shadowing

Job-shadowing is not sufficient by itself, especially if you only do it for a day, because the attorney(s) you're shadowing will feel pressure to show you only the most interesting stuff. Plus, people under observation act differently, a phenomenon psychologists call "reactivity."[78] Still, job-shadowing might be helpful as an supplemental strategy if you're trying to scope out different work environments. The best way to set this up is either through people you already know, like a friend's parent, or as a next-level step after you've done an informational interview with someone.

When you're job-shadowing, see if you like the people. Remember, you'd be spending a *lot* of time with these people, so if the culture isn't for you, that matters. Ask them about the cases they're on and what kind of work they're doing. Do they seem excited about their work? Are *you* excited about their work?

If all else fails, go back to the questions you'd ask during an informational interview to get a better sense of what it's like to work there. The advantage of job-shadowing is that there will be a lot more people to ask! It's a red flag if you're only able to speak to a couple of people, because that means: (a) people aren't friendly with one another, (b) they're

---

[78] Jason G. Goldman,"How Being Watched Changes You – Without You Knowing," *BBC,* February 10, 2014, http://www.bbc.com/future/story /20140209-being-watched-why-thats-good; Sander van der Linden, "How the Illusion of Being Observed Can Make You a Better Person," *Scientific American*, May 3, 2011, http://www.scientificamerican.com /article/how-the-illusion-of-being-observed-can-make-you-better -person/.

too busy or self-important to make time for you, and/or (c) management doesn't trust them to say nice things about the company.

Honorable mentions

In addition to talking with lawyers in real life, there are a few other resources worth looking at.

Above the Law. The blog Above the Law is like *Gossip Girl* for lawyers. ATL reveals what lawyers find interesting and important in a non-boring-law-review way. Law firms worry about what ATL will say about them. Law students are addicted to it. Need I say more?

Law reviews and journals. Aside from ATL, take a look at law reviews and other law journals[79] — you can find a list of them by topic on Wikipedia. Reading law journals will help you broaden your horizons about what types of law are out there and what kinds of issues lawyers find significant. If you genuinely find the journals interesting and want to read and discuss such things for fun, you have my blessing to go to law school.

---

[79] As a refresher, law review is basically a law school's most elite law journal (and possibly the only one, if the school is small).

Part Five:

Next Steps

Chapter 15:
If You Still Want to Go to Law School

If you've skipped the rest of this book to go straight to this chapter because you "already know you want to go to law school," you're doing it wrong. Start at the beginning. (That's why it's the beginning.)

Ahem. Now back to our regularly scheduled programming.

Before you commit

Before you commit to going to law school, I need you to do a few things first.

First, make sure you followed the advice in Chapter 14 (Now Do Your Research) about talking to lawyers in real life. If you haven't talked to at least three lawyers, you're not ready to go to law school. If you're willing to get thousands of dollars in debt for law school, you should be willing to spend a couple of hours making sure it's actually what you want to do.

Second, I want you to take a few minutes and write about why you want to go to law school. I know, this feels like an obnoxious school essay assignment, especially since you already did the personal mission statement, but trust me, freewriting has a way of making you realize things that were hidden in your subconscious. In fact, I came up with the idea for this book while doing a freewriting exercise, even though the thought had never crossed my mind before. So don't underestimate its power.

Now set a timer for five minutes, and start writing. If the timer goes off and you're not done, keep going. (Conversely, if you're having trouble articulating why you want to go to law school, that itself should be a red flag.)

In *Stumbling on Happiness*, Daniel Gilbert asserts that the best way to figure out if something will make you happy is to look at whether it has made *other* people happy, because that has been shown to be a more reliable indicator than how happy you think it will make you.[80] But, as he laments, "we think of ourselves as unique entities—minds unlike any others—and thus we often reject the lessons that the emotional experience of others has to teach us."[81]

With that in mind, ask yourself: Do you sound more like the people who left, or the people who stayed?

---

[80] Daniel Gilbert, *Stumbling on Happiness* (New York: Vintage Books, 2006), 245-257.

[81] Gilbert, 257.

Going to law school is only worthwhile if...

Most of the lawyers I interviewed agreed that you should go to a top school and/or a school in the region where you want to practice. Eliza asserts that you should go to a top-20 school if you can get in; if you can't, you should at least have a decent scholarship to a school in the geographic region where you want to practice. Otherwise, she says, "you'll be wasting time and money, and you're going to be unhappy, because you'll be in debt forever."

I'm sure many of you will want to argue the specific ranking cutoff in terms of what constitutes a top school, but you're missing the point. Bottom line, you know what a top school is, because you've actually heard of it. And bear in mind that if you want a job in, e.g., Boston, you're going to be competing with Harvard kids. Or if it's New York, NYU and Columbia. In Philly, it's Penn.

Basically, if there's a top school in the area where you want to work, and you don't go there, it's going to be a tough sell.

Also, do *not* rely on employment statistics in deciding where or whether to go to law school. Law schools will do anything to inflate their numbers — there have literally been lawsuits over this[82]. And unfortunately, the American Bar Association (ABA) has waffled over the last few years about how much transparency to require in law schools' employment reporting.

For a while, beginning around 2011,[83] the ABA required law schools to provide more transparency, including identifying jobs funded by the law school itself (a time-honored tactic for gaming the stats) and non-legal jobs (like working at Starbucks, which law schools were totally including). But in 2017, the ABA reversed course, combining a bunch of different employment categories,[84] and allowing law schools to count positions they were funding as "full-time employment" as long as the schools paid over $40,000

---

[82] Scott Jaschik, "Suing Over Jobs," *Inside Higher Ed*, August 11, 2011, https://www.insidehighered.com/news/2011/08/11/suits_challenge _veracity_of_job_placement_rates_at_3_law_schools; Staci Zaretsky, "Verdict Reached in the Alaburda v. Thomas Jefferson Law Landmark Case over Fraudulent Employment Statistics," *Above the Law*, March 24, 2016, https://abovethelaw.com/2016/03/a-verdict-has-been-reached-in-the -alaburda-v-thomas-jefferson-school-of-law-landmark-case-over -fraudulent-employment-statistics/.

[83] Kyle McEntee, "The Fall of Systemic Deception at Law Schools,"*Above the Law*. March 29, 2016, https://abovethelaw.com/2016/03/the-fall -of-systemic-deception-at-law-schools/.

[84] Kyle McEntee, "ABA Takes Giant Step Backwards on Transparency," *Above the Law*. August 3, 2017, https://abovethelaw.com/2017/08/aba -takes-giant-step-backwards-on-transparency/.

and the job lasted more than one year.[85] Not exactly confidence-inspiring.

Anyway, even if you think you want to stay in your (non-metropolitan) region, you should still go to the best school possible. You just never know what can happen in life. For instance, you may meet someone in law school and fall in love, but then find out that they need to be in North Dakota to be close to their ill relative. Or maybe the position that you thought was your dream job just isn't. So even if you think you know what you want, you owe it to yourself to make sure you have as many doors open as possible. And the only way to do that is to go to, for lack of a better term, a "name-brand" school like Harvard, Yale, or Stanford.

"But what if I can't get into Harvard?" you ask. I won't say, "Then don't go to law school," because I believe that there's too much emphasis put on the prestige of your law school and not enough on whether you've developed the skills actually needed to be an effective lawyer.

But (you knew there'd be a "but"), that makes it even more imperative that you figure out exactly what you want before you get to law school. First, that will help you determine whether what you want is even feasible. There's

---

[85] Stephanie Francis Ward, "ABA Legal Ed Council Will Talk More About How Law School-Funded Jobs Get Reported," *ABA Journal*, August 7, 2017, http://www.abajournal.com/news/article/aba_legal_education _council_law_school_funded_employment_questionnaire.

no point in going to law school if you can only get into Podunk Law School and you want to work as White House Counsel. Second, knowing what you want clarifies what you need to excel at in order to achieve your goals. Remember, the worse the school is, the better you have to do to be marketable, and it's not that easy when everyone at the lower-tier schools knows that that's what they have to do.

Long story short, if you can't get into a top school and you don't have a clear sense of what you want to do, don't go to law school until you have one or the other.

By the way, this is all true even if Mom and Dad are paying (unless your parents have their own law firm and you actually want to go there after graduation). Sure, you won't be weighed down with student loans, but you'll also have just wasted three years of your life. Remember what I said about opportunity costs, not to mention the other non-financial "costs" of law school.

If you do get into Harvard or Yale or Stanford, congratulations! That still doesn't mean that you have to go to law school — you get bragging rights even if you don't go. But if you *are* considering it, here's the (purely anecdotal) inside scoop on those schools:

- **Harvard.** Described by many as a "pressure-cooker," students here are probably the most miserable of the three. I'm not sure why. Maybe because the school is so big, you have to fight to distinguish yourself? But you do get to say you go to Harvard, the same school attended by Barack and Michelle Obama, Tom Cruise's character in *A Few Good Men*, and Elle Woods from *Legally Blonde*.

- **Yale.** Students here might be happier, but they don't actually learn anything practical. It's all theory taught by academics.

- **Stanford.** Stanford students seem genuinely happy, presumably due to the sunshine. I'll be honest, if I had to go to law school all over again, I'd probably go to Stanford if I could get in. Although I did hear that Stanford is where the term "duck syndrome" originated...

If you're thinking, "I want to do public interest work, I don't have to worry about any of that stuff," think again. Public interest work, despite paying next to nothing, is actually pretty competitive, especially if you want to go a high-profile organization like the American Civil Liberties Union (ACLU).

Also, despite your current intent to do public interest work, the odds are very good that you'll nonetheless go to a firm after graduation. It's not your fault; the institutional forces of law school push you to go that way.[86] And since

---

[86] *See* Chapter 8 (Working at a Big Law Firm).

you're already on the path of, well, following the path, it's all too easy to keep going the way they want you to.

Like I said, I initially wanted to do civil rights work, but my interest wasn't strong enough to prevent me from being funneled to a firm. So you have to *really* want it. And you can only really want it if you have concrete, real-world experience in your area of interest. "Concrete" means volunteering with a real-life organization that does the type of work you think you're interested in; it does not mean doing a couple of Mock Trial cases in that area of law. Learn from my mistakes, don't repeat them!

Take time off

Okay, so you've decided you really, truly want to go law school. Good job. You should still take *at least* one year off to work, whether in the law or elsewhere.

"But *why?*" you ask, exasperated. "I wrote my personal mission statement, I did all that networking crap, and now I want to go law school more than ever. So what's the point in waiting?"

I appreciate your enthusiasm, but you're not a Jedi yet. First, there's no need to freak out, as most schools let you defer for a year or two for almost any reason after they admit you. Basically, you can eat your cake and have it too.

Second, the aim of taking time off is to develop your identity outside of school so that you're less likely to let law school define you. Working enables you to become a person, not just a student. You've been judged and defined by grades for the majority of your life, and it's going to destroy you if you let that define you in law school.

Or, as Julie aptly put it, "You can't see through the law school track bullshit unless you've taken time off."

By the "law school track," she meant the path of what you're "supposed" to do in law school: be on a law journal, preferably law review; apply for federal clerkships, and aim for appellate because it's more prestigious, even if you'd rather do trial work; go to a big law firm because it's prestigious and pays a lot; and on and on. "You need to make conscious decisions," she points out. Without time in the real world to develop your own sense of self, one independent from your parents and school and all the rest of it, it's all too easy to just follow the herd.

One of my biggest regrets is not taking a year or more off to work between college and law school. Not only did I feel defined by my suddenly mediocre grades in law school, but working at a law firm after I graduated was not pretty. It's overwhelming to have a law firm gig as your first "real" job because it demands so much more from you than a normal job.

Plus, working full-time at a normal job beforehand gives you an opportunity to learn the unwritten rules of the workplace and how to be a professional, which you simply can't learn in school. If you already have that foundation when you go to law school, you'll be much better equipped to deal with all the other stuff that you'll need to learn and deal with as a practicing lawyer. Conversely, if you don't have that foundation, it's harder to see how unreasonable and bizarre many legal offices are, which in turn makes it harder for you to figure out what you do and don't have to put up with at work.

Finally, if nothing else, having work experience looks good on your resume. Employers are much more likely to hire you if they know you can handle working in the real world. You've probably heard complaints from older folks about younger generations being "entitled." While I think there are a few factors at play there, probably one of the biggest is that a lot of law students, especially at the elite schools, haven't worked for any meaningful period of time. But luckily, this is changing.[87] Don't get left behind.

---

[87] Andrew H. Duehren, "Law School Admissions 'Actively Preferences' Work Experience," *Harvard Crimson*, April 9, 2015, http://www.thecrimson .com/article/2015/4/9/hls-admissions-work-experience/; Maya Itah, "Northwestern Law Dean: Never Let a Good Crisis Go to Waste," *Fortune*, June 9, 2014, https://fortune.com/2014/06/09/northwestern -law-dean-never-let-a-good-crisis-go-to-waste/ (noting that "Northwestern began putting a strong emphasis on work experience about a dozen years ago" and discussing the reasons why).

Chapter 16: How to Break the News

Okay, so you've made the smart decision not to go to law school, or at least delay it for a while. Now let's talk about how to break the "bad" news to your parents and anyone else trying to get you to go to law school...

1. Prepare

Before you have The Talk, you need to prepare yourself.

Write about your anxieties. First, I want you to write about your anxieties. Your anxieties regarding your family's reaction, your anxieties about what you're going to do next — basically everything causing you anxiety about this new path. You might even do it in multiple writing sessions, with a different focus each time.

I'm suggesting you do this because writing about your anxieties has been shown to reduce them and improve performance.[88] Granted, most of the studies have been done in an academic environment, where performance was measured as grades on the test. But I think the takeaway is the same here.

---

[88] *See, e.g.*, Ramirez, Gerardo, and Sian L. Beilock. "Writing About Testing Worries Boosts Exam Performance in the Classroom." *Science* 331, no. 6014 (January 14, 2011).

See a therapist. It's also a good idea to see a therapist, if you're not already. You've probably been living a long time with the concrete, well-laid identity as a lawyer-to-be. Now you're faced with taking on a scary, nebulous identity as someone who's not sure what they want to be/do. As a bonus, your therapist can help you role-play having the conversation with your parents.

Bear in mind that you might have to meet with a few different therapists before you find one who's a good fit. But it's worth the effort, because you'll get way more out of it. Therapy can be challenging even when you've been doing it for a while, so make sure you're working with someone you like and respect. (And if you do end up going to law school, you'll definitely want a good therapist.)

Review your personal mission statement. Your personal mission statement serves multiple purposes: it helps ground you when you waver or feel lost, it gives you something polished to present to your family, and it allows you to "edit" your story in a way that gives you back the control you might have felt you lost when law school stopped being a given. So make sure it's at the front of your mind when you talk to them.

Extra credit. I also recommend going through a few career books and informational interviews before you talk to your parents for a few reasons. First, it's further evidence that you've taken the initiative in figuring out the rest of your life.

Second, your parents will likely panic in seeing that you're starting to deviate from the law school path. Panic translates to, out of good intentions, doing their best to cause you to doubt yourself so that you'll go back to the "safe" path of law school. But if you already have your wheels in motion down another path, it'll be way harder to dissuade you.

Third, going through this process has hopefully helped you narrow down what you're looking for, so you can offer some concrete alternatives to law school when your parents inevitably ask you what you're going to do instead.

Finally, doing informational interviews puts you in a better position when you're ready to actually start looking for a job. Why? Because 60-80% of job openings are filled through networking.[89] So you'll be grateful to have those connections when the rest of your classmates are wildly applying to the same jobs.

---

[89] *See, e.g.,* Kimberly Beatty, "The Math Behind the Networking Claim," *Jobfully Blog,* July 1, 2010, https://blog.jobfully.com/2010/07/the-math-behind-the-networking-claim/; Emily Driscoll, "It's All About Who You Know: Networking to Get a Job," *Fox Business,* March 4, 2016, http://www.foxbusiness.com/features/its-all-about-who-you-know-networking-to-get-a-job; Lisa Amin Gulezian, "Hundreds of Jobs Offered at Job Fair," *ABC7 News,* May 24, 2011, http://abc7news.com/archive/8149633/.

2. The Talk

Now that you're ready for The Talk, there are a few things you should keep in mind going in.

A. It's going to suck. First, accept that it's going to be difficult. You probably didn't end up on the path to law school by yourself, and whatever the reason your family wants you to go to law school, they will not be happy with your announcement. **That's okay.** Standing up for yourself in the face of what your parents are trying to pressure you into is a critical milestone on the road to becoming an independent adult. You should be proud of yourself.

B. Your approach. With that in mind, let's talk about the approach. I suggest saying something like, "I wanted to let you know that I've decided to wait to go to law school until I've worked for a while first."

There are a few things to note about this phrasing. First, it omits any mention of a timeframe. You don't want to have your parents calling you in a year and saying, "Well, the one year is up! Now, about law school..."

Second, saying "I've decided" makes it clear that it's a done deal, instead of saying something like "I'm thinking about...", where your parents would get the impression that you're still unsure and therefore open to, shall we say, persuasion. Don't get me wrong, they'll try to change your mind anyway, but at least you're starting off strong.

Third, "I've decided to wait" is sufficiently ambiguous that it leaves the door open for either going to law school in the future or not, depending on what you end up choosing.

Fourth, phrasing it as, "I wanted to let you know that I've decided" communicates that you're taking charge of your career. And to drive the point home further, you've got your mission statement and the other actions you've taken to show that you're not just muddling along.

C. Their reaction. Here are some of the questions/reactions you're likely to get:

Reaction #1: "What?? Where is this coming from?"

Your response: "I've been researching the legal profession to get a better idea of what I want to do, and it seems like it might not be as good a fit as I thought. I want to make sure that law school is the right choice before I get into hundreds of thousands of dollars in debt." If your parents are like mine, once you get them to focus on the debt rather than the prestige, they'll come around more quickly.

If your parents are paying and/or that reason seems too fluffy or otherwise insufficient, you can add, "Plus, the best law schools prefer students with work experience," and then show them the Harvard article I referenced earlier in this chapter.[90] This reason should be a ringer, since your parents want you to go to the best school and have the best employment opportunities after. Nothing but the best for you, kiddo!

Reaction #2: "So what are you going to do instead? You can't just live at home forever."

Your response: Whip out the research you've been doing, along with your mission statement and plan of action. "My plan is to find a job in [this industry], which I think would be a good fit for [reasons]. In fact, I've already reached out to [people in that area] to learn more."

Reaction #3: "If you start working, you'll never go back to school."

Your response: I think there are a few different things going on with this one. First, they might be concerned that you'll lose momentum. But you can alleviate those fears by re-framing it as an intentional part of your plan, rather than a "break." That way, you go from an aimless drifter mooching off your parents to a prudent adult who's thinking ahead.

Alternatively, they might be worried that once you get used to making money, you won't want to go back to school, where the flow of money abruptly stops and starts going in

---

[90] Andrew H. Duehren, "Law School Admissions 'Actively Preferences' Work Experience," *Harvard Crimson*, April 9, 2015, http://www.thecrimson.com/article/2015/4/9/hls-admissions-work-experience/.

the other direction. And honestly, there's no way to know until you're in the situation. But I think that, if you really want to go to law school, you'll figure it out.

Moreover, it's become common to leave jobs after a year or two, and even more so to go back to school. In fact, most business schools, including Harvard, require that you work first. It's mystifying that law school should be any different. Indeed, there is increasing emphasis, at least in law firms, that law is a business. Therefore, as far as I'm concerned, law school should be treated accordingly.

D. Your life's work. If you're still struggling with telling your parents or other loved ones, remember this: At the end of the day, it's your life. Period.

The most common regret of the people on their deathbed is, "I wish I'd had the courage to live a life true to myself, not the life others expected of me."[91]

So you have to decide what your life is worth to you.

---

[91] Joe Martino, "The Top 5 Regrets of the Dying," *Huffington Post*, August 3, 2013, https://www.huffingtonpost.com/2013/08/03/top-5-regrets -of-the-dying_n_3640593.html.

Conclusion: Looking Back

When I was about to graduate Harvard Law School, the school asked us to fill out a survey. One of the questions was: "If I could go back, would I go to law school again?"

The short answer is probably not. The longer answer is that I regret my decision to go to law school mostly because I had no idea what I was getting myself into.

Luckily, you get to avoid all that through this book. You're welcome.

References

Books

Burnett, Bill and Dave Evans. *Designing Your Life*. New York: Alfred A. Knopf, 2016.

Collins, Jim. *Good to Great: Why Some Companies Make the Leap... and Others Don't*. New York: HarperCollins, 2001.

Covey, Stephen R. *The 7 Habits of Highly Effective People: Powerful Lessons in Personal Change*. 25th anniversary ed. New York: Simon & Schuster, 2004.

Gilbert, Daniel. *Stumbling on Happiness*. New York: Vintage Books, 2006.

Goldstein, Noah J., Steve J. Martin, and Robert B. Cialdini. *Yes! 50 Scientifically Proven Ways to Be Persuasive*. New York: Free Press, 2008.

Lyubomirsky, Sonja. *The How of Happiness: A New Approach to Getting the Life You Want*. New York: Penguin Books, 2007.

Mertz, Elizabeth. *The Language of Law School: Learning to 'Think Like a Lawyer'*. New York: Oxford University Press, 2007.

McGonigal, Kelly. *The Willpower Instinct: How Self-Control Works, Why It Matters, and What You Can Do to Get More of It*. New York: Avery, 2012.

Pink, Daniel H. *Drive: The Surprising Truth About What Motivates Us.* New York: Riverhead Books, 2009.

Rath, Tom. *StrengthFinders 2.0.* New York: Gallup, 2007.

Young, Kathryne. *How to Be Sort of Happy in Law School.* Stanford: Stanford University Press, 2018.

Journal Articles

Arndt, Jamie, Jeff Schimel, Jeff Greenberg, and Tom Pyszczynski. "The Intrinsic Self and Defensiveness: Evidence That Activating the Intrinsic Self Reduces Self-Handicapping and Conformity." *Personality and Social Psychology Bulletin* 28, no. 5 (May 2002): 671-683.

Barkai, John, Elizabeth Kent, and Pamela Martin. "A Profile of Settlement." *Court Review: The Journal of the American Judges Association* 42, no. 3 (December 2006): 34-39.

Baumeister, Roy F. "Suicide as Escape From Self." *Psychological Review* 97, no. 1 (January 1990): 90-113.

Benjamin, G. Andrew H., Alfred Kazsniak, Bruce Sales, and Stephen B. Shanfield. "The Role of Legal Education in Producing Psychological Distress Among Law Students and Lawyers." *American Bar Foundation Research Journal* 11, no. 2 (Spring 1986): 225-252.

Eaton, William W., James C. Anthony, Wallace Mandel, and Roberta Garrison. "Occupations and the Prevalence of

Major Depressive Disorder." *Journal of Occupational Medicine* 32, no. 11 (Nov. 1990): 1079-1087.

Floyd, Daisy Hurst. "We Can Do More." *Journal of Legal Education* 60, no. 1 (August 2010): 129-134.

King, Laura A. "The Health Benefits of Writing About Life Goals." *Personality and Social Psychology Bulletin* 27, no. 7 (July 2001): 798-807.

Krill, Patrick R., Ryan Johnson, and Linda Albert. "The Prevalence of Substance Use and Other Mental Health Concerns Among American Attorneys." *Journal of Addiction Medicine* 10, no. 1 (January/February 2016): 46-52.

Masicampo, E. J., and Roy F. Baumeister. "Consider It Done! Plan Making Can Eliminate the Cognitive Effects of Unfulfilled Goals." *Journal of Personality and Social Psychology* 101, no. 4 (October 2011): 667-683.

O'Brien, Molly Townes, Stephen Tang, and Kath Hall. "Changing Our Thinking: Empirical Research on Law Student Wellbeing, Thinking Styles and the Law Curriculum." *Legal Education Review* 21, no. 2 (January 2011): 149-182.

Oreskovich, Michael R., Krista L. Kaups, Charles M. Balch, et al. "Prevalence of Alcohol Use Disorders Among American Surgeons." *Arch Surgery* 147, no. 2 (2012): 168-174.

Parade, Stuart L. "Bill, Baby, Bill: How the Billable Hour Emerged as the Primary Method of Attorney Fee Generation and Why Early Reports of Its Demise May Be Greatly Exaggerated." *Idaho Law Review* 50, no. 1 (2013).

Ramirez, Gerardo, and Sian L. Beilock. "Writing About Testing Worries Boosts Exam Performance in the Classroom." *Science* 331, no. 6014 (January 14, 2011): 211-213.

Rhode, Deborah L. "Legal Education: Professional Interests and Public Values." *Indiana Law Review* 34 (2000): 23-45.

Robinson, Nick. "The Decline of the Lawyer-Politician." *Buffalo Law Review* 65, no. 4 (August 2017): 657-737.

Schlegel, Rebecca J., Joshua A. Hicks, Jamie Arndt, and Laura A. King. "Thine Own Self: True Self-Concept Accessibility and Meaning in Life." *Journal of Personality and Social Psychology* 96, no. 2 (2009): 473-490.

Schlegel, Rebecca J., Joshua A. Hicks, Laura A. King, and Jamie Arndt. "Feeling Like You Know Who You Are: Perceived True Self-Knowledge and Meaning in Life." *Personality and Social Psychology Bulletin* 37, no. 6 (March 2011): 745-756.

Sheldon, Kennon M., and Lawrence S. Krieger. "Does Legal Education Have Undermining Effects on Law Students? Evaluating Changes in Motivation, Values, and Well-Being." *Behavioral Sciences and the Law* 22 (2004): 261-286.

Sweet, Elizabeth, Arijit Nandi, Emma K. Adam, and Thomas W. McDade. "The High Price of Debt: Household Financial Debt and Its Impact on Mental and Physical Health." *Social Science & Medicine* 91 (August 2013): 94-100.

Walsemann, Katrina M., Gilbert C. Gee, and Danielle Gentile. "Sick of Our Loans: Student Borrowing and the Mental Health of Young Adults in the United States." *Social Science & Medicine* 124 (January 2015): 85-93.

Online Resources

2021 Legal Trends Report. Clio, 2021. https://www.clio.com/wp-content/uploads/2021/08/2021-Legal-Trends-Report-Oct-26.pdf.

Achor, Shawn, Gabriella Rosen Kellerman, Andrew Reece, and Alexi Robichaux. "America's Loneliest Workers, According to Research." *Harvard Business Review.* March 19, 2018. https://hbr.org/2018/03/americas-loneliest-workers-according-to-research.

Amin Gulezian, Lisa. "Hundreds of Jobs Offered at Job Fair." *ABC7 News.* May 24, 2011. http://abc7news.com/archive/8149633/.

Barker, Eric. *Barking Up the Wrong Tree* (blog). https://www.bakadesuyo.com/.

Beatty, Kimberly. "The Math Behind the Networking Claim." *Jobfully Blog*. July 1, 2010. https://blog.jobfully.com/2010/07/the-math-behind-the-networking-claim/.

Berman, Casey. "My 21 Step Guide on How to Leave the Law and Begin Anew." *Leave Law Behind*. April 23, 2015. http://leavelawbehind.com/2015/04/23/my-21-step-guide-on-how-to-leave-the-law-and-begin-anew/.

Berman, Casey. "Thinking (or Not Thinking) Critically." *Leave Law Behind*. April 26, 2010. http://leavelawbehind.com/2010/04/26/thinking-or-not-thinking-critically/.

Berman, Casey. "The Third Step in Leaving Law Behind – Do What You Are Good At." *Leave Law Behind*. March 29, 2013. http://leavelawbehind.com/2013/03/29/the-third-step-in-leaving-law-behind-do-what-you-are-good-at/.

Berman, Casey. "A Valuable Lesson from Last Week's Leave Law Behind Event." *Leave Law Behind*. October 8, 2012. http://leavelawbehind.com/2012/10/08/a-valuable-lesson-from-last-weeks-leave-law-behind-event/.

Cassens Weiss, Debra. "Lawyers Rank Highest on 'Loneliness Scale,' Study Finds." *ABA Journal*, April 3, 2018. http://www.abajournal.com/news/article/lawyers_rank_highest_on_loneliness_scale_study_finds/.

Chamorro-Premuzic, Tomas. "Does Money Really Affect Motivation? A Review of the Research." *Harvard Business Review*. April 10, 2013. https://hbr.org/2013/04/does-money-really-affect-motiv.

Cho, Jeena. "How to Know Suicide." *Above the Law*. March 31, 2015. http://abovethelaw.com/2015/03/how-to-know-suicide/.

Driscoll, Emily. "It's All About Who You Know: Networking to Get a Job." *Fox Business*. March 4, 2016. http://www.foxbusiness.com/features/its-all-about-who-you-know-networking-to-get-a-job.

Duehren, Andrew H. "Law School Admissions 'Actively Preferences' Work Experience." *Harvard Crimson*. April 9, 2015. http://www.thecrimson.com/article/2015/4/9/hls-admissions-work-experience/.

Elefant, Carolyn. "When #Altlaw Is Bad, It Is Truly Horrid." *Above the Law*. February 22, 2018. https://abovethelaw.com/2018/02/when-altlaw-is-bad-it-is-truly-horrid/.

"FAQs – General Information." Supreme Court of the United States (website). Accessed July 4, 2018. https://www.supremecourt.gov/about/faq_general.aspx.

Francis Ward, Stephanie. "ABA Legal Ed Council Will Talk More About How Law School-Funded Jobs Get Reported." *ABA Journal.* August 7, 2017. http://www.abajournal.com/news/article/aba_legal _education_council_law_school_funded_employment _questionnaire.

Goldman, Jason G. "How Being Watched Changes You – Without You Knowing." *BBC.* February 10, 2014. http://www.bbc.com/future/story/20140209-being -watched-why-thats-good.

Gramlich, John. "Only 2% of Federal Criminal Defendants Go to Trial, and Most Who Do Are Found Guilty." *Pew Research Center.* June 11, 2019. https://www.pewresearch.org/fact -tank/2019/06/11/only-2-of-federal-criminal-defendants -go-to-trial-and-most-who-do-are-found-guilty/.

Haden, Jeff. "How 1 Missing Comma Just Cost This Company $5 Million (But Did Make Its Employees $5 Million Richer)." *Inc.com,* February 12, 2018. https://www.inc.com/jeff -haden/how-1-missing-comma-just-cost-this-company-5 -million-but-did-make-its-employees-5-million-richer.html.

Itah, Maya. "Northwestern Law Dean: Never Let a Good Crisis Go to Waste." *Fortune.* June 9, 2014. https://fortune.com /2014/06/09/northwestern-law-dean-never-let-a-good-crisis -go-to-waste/.

Jaschik, Scott. "Suing Over Jobs." *Inside Higher Ed.* August 11, 2011. https://www.insidehighered.com/news/2011/08/11/suits_challenge_veracity_of_job_placement_rates_at_3_law_schools.

Johnson, Kristin. "Investigative Report: Mental Health and Substance Abuse Threaten the Legal Profession." *Rocket Matter.* March 12, 2018. https://www.rocketmatter.com/attorney-wellness/investigative-report-mental-health-substance-abuse-threaten-legal-profession/.

Korkki, Phyllis. "Job Satisfaction vs. a Big Paycheck." *New York Times.* September 11, 2010. http://www.nytimes.com/2010/09/12/jobs/12search.html.

Martino, Joe. "The Top 5 Regrets of the Dying." *Huffington Post.* August 3, 2013. https://www.huffingtonpost.com/2013/08/03/top-5-regrets-of-the-dying_n_3640593.html.

McEntee, Kyle. "ABA Takes Giant Step Backwards on Transparency." *Above the Law.* August 3, 2017. https://abovethelaw.com/2017/08/aba-takes-giant-step-backwards-on-transparency/.

McEntee, Kyle. "The Fall of Systemic Deception at Law Schools." *Above the Law.* March 29, 2016. https://abovethelaw.com/2016/03/the-fall-of-systemic-deception-at-law-schools/.

McMullan Abrams, Leigh. "The Only Job with an Industry Devoted to Helping People Quit." *The Atlantic.* July 29, 2014. https://www.theatlantic.com/business/archive/2014/07/the-only-job-with-an-industry-devoted-to-helping-people-quit/375199/.

Moon, Susan. "9 Things That May Surprise You About Going In-House." *Above the Law.* June 10, 2014. http://abovethelaw.com/2014/06/9-things-that-may-surprise-you-about-going-in-house/.

Moon, Susan. "Moonlighting: Things Not to Say In-House – 'I'm Bad at Math'." *Above the Law.* January 6, 2012. http://abovethelaw.com/2012/01/moonlighting-things-not-to-say-in-house-im-bad-at-math/.

Meyerhofer, Will. "Why You're So Unhappy." *The People's Therapist.* November 4, 2015. https://thepeoplestherapist.com/2015/11/04/why-youre-so-unhappy/.

Mystal, Elie. "Justice Antonin Scalia Says Some of the Best Minds May Be Wasted on Law." *Above the Law.* October 1, 2009. https://abovethelaw.com/2009/10/justice-antonin-scalia-says-some-of-the-best-minds-may-be-wasted-on-law/.

Mystal, Elie. "Quinn Emanuel Believes in 'C.B.A.' (Check BlackBerry Always)." *Above the Law.* October 16, 2009. http://abovethelaw.com/2009/10/quinn-emanuel-believes-in-c-b-a-check-blackberry-always/.

"Report: Guilty Pleas on the Rise, Criminal Trials on the Decline." *Innocence Project.* August 7, 2018. https://www.innocenceproject.org/guilty-pleas-on-the-rise-criminal-trials-on-the-decline/.

Saksa, Jim. "'You Can Do Anything With a Law Degree.'" *Slate.* May 14, 2014. https://slate.com/human-interest/2014/05/you-can-do-anything-with-a-law-degree-no-no-you-cannot.html.

Van der Linden, Sander. "How the Illusion of Being Observed Can Make You a Better Person." *Scientific American.* May 3, 2011. http://www.scientificamerican.com/article/how-the-illusion-of-being-observed-can-make-you-better-person/.

Watkins, Simon. "Typing Error Cost Lockheed Pounds 43M." *The Independent,* June 19, 1999. https://www.independent.co.uk/news/typing-error-cost-lockheed-pounds-43m-1100991.html.

Watson Peláez, Marina. "Plan Your Way to Less Stress, More Happiness." *TIME.com.* May 31, 2011. http://healthland.time.com/2011/05/31/study-25-of-happiness-depends-on-stress-management/.

Zaretsky, Staci. "Verdict Reached in the Alaburda v. Thomas Jefferson Law Landmark Case over Fraudulent Employment Statistics." *Above the Law.* March 24, 2016. https://abovethelaw.com/2016/03/a-verdict-has-been-reached-in-the-alaburda-v-thomas-jefferson-school-of-law-landmark-case-over-fraudulent-employment-statistics/.

Acknowledgements

Without the awesome folks at Self-Publishing School, you would not be reading this book. They provided the tools to help me get it written, and then to get it published.

I also owe a debt of gratitude to all the current and former lawyers who agreed to be interviewed. While not every interview made it onto these pages, it was invaluable to get everyone's perspectives and insights into the strange and special world of law.

Thank you to my editor and friend, Holly Bowers, for your gentle yet critical edits to the draft I wrote soon after leaving law, when I was still in my feelings.

Thank you to my friend Liz, who provided much-needed feedback and cheerleading in the home stretch.

Finally, a special thanks to my husband, Adam. He puts up with a lot.